Show What You Know® on the 7th Grade WASL

Student Workbook

by:
Kevin D. Arnold, Ph.D.
Sheila LaSalle
Kimberly P. Mattson, M.A.

Published by:
Show What You Know® Publishing
A Division of Englefield & Associates, Inc.
P.O. Box 341348
Columbus, OH 43234-1348
614-764-1211

www.showwhatyouknowpublishing.com

Printed in the United States of America
05 04 03 02   20 19 18 17 16 15 14 13 12 11 10 9 8 7 6 5 4 3 2 1

ISBN: 1-884183-51-4

About the Authors

Kevin D. Arnold, Ph.D., is a psychologist and Director of the Center for Cognitive and Behavioral Therapy in Columbus, Ohio. He received his Masters and Doctorate degrees in developmental psychology from The Ohio State University, where he served as a faculty member, researcher, and administrator in The Ohio State University College of Education. He is a Diplomate with the American Board of Professional Psychology, holds advanced certificates in Cognitive Behavioral Therapy, and is President of the Ohio Psychological Association. Dr. Arnold is the contributing author of the Test-Taking Strategies and Test Anxiety chapters of this book.

Sheila LaSalle is a teacher at Eastgate Elementary School in Kennewick, Washington. She received a Bachelor's degree in Elementary Education from Eastern Washington University with endorsements in reading and math. She has twelve years of teaching experience, and is currently a reading specialist with English as a Second Language students and at-risk students. She has created and presented thematic units for her district as well as for her local educational service district. In addition to this book, Sheila is published in the *Journal of Educational Counselors*. She is the contributing author for the Mathematics chapter of this book.

Kimberly P. Mattson, M.A., is a seventh grade teacher at Horse Heaven Hills Middle School in Kennewick, Washington. She has worked in the Kennewick School District for 15 years, nine years as a fourth grade teacher and six years as a seventh grade Reading, Language Arts, and Social Studies teacher. She received her master's degree in Curriculum and Instruction from Eastern Washington University. Kim was granted a two-year professional leave of absence to serve as a teacher on special assignment for Educational Service District 123. As the Literacy Specialist, she provided customized staff development in Reading, Writing, and Communication with an emphasis on aligning instruction with the Essential Academic Learning Requirements for Washington State. Kim Mattson is the contributing author of three chapters in this book: Reading, Writing, and Listening.

Acknowledgements

Show What You Know® Publishing acknowledges the following for their efforts in making this assessment material available for Washington students, parents, and teachers:

Cindi Englefield, President/Publisher
Eloise Boehm-Sasala, Vice President/Managing Editor
Mercedes Baltzell, Production Editor
Bethany Hansgen, Project Editor
Scott D. Stuckey, Project Editor
Jennifer King, Illustrator/Cover Designer

Chapter Proofreaders:

Erica T. Klingerman
Phyllis Y. Keiley-Tyler

Test Anxiety

Reduce Your Nervous Feelings About Taking Tests

Does the thought of taking the Washington Assessment of Student Learning (WASL) make you nervous or scared? If so, you're not alone. Being nervous about any kind of test is a normal feeling that many students experience. The nervous feeling you have about things is called *anxiety*. A small amount of test anxiety is common, but it is important **not** to let it affect how you feel about taking the WASL. This chapter was written to help you control nervous and anxious feelings, and let you show what you know® on the WASL.

There are a number of things you will notice about your feelings or actions if you are afraid of the WASL. For one thing, you might feel things physically. For example, when studying for the WASL, you might get a headache. You might also find your usual behaviors are changing, such as not being able to sleep at night, or becoming upset or cranky. You might begin to ignore the WASL, pretend it won't occur, or try to avoid any talk about it. Another thing you might notice if you're nervous is your mind working differently. If this occurs, you may have trouble concentrating when you take the WASL, and you might find it hard to think clearly or remember things you know very well.

If you have any of these signs to a degree that is unusually high for you, or if you have these problems much more so than most students your age, you might be overly nervous about the WASL. This chapter will help you overcome your nervous feelings so you can do your best when the time comes to take the WASL.

Understanding Fear of Taking Tests

Fear of anything, the WASL included, is a reaction to a situation or event that you believe to be dangerous or that you think might cause you harm. Usually, you will experience fear when you cannot avoid the situation and, therefore, must deal with it.

For example, if you must go to school and present a project to your class, and you believe you will do a bad job, people will laugh at you, you will fail the presentation, and you will be grounded (all of which can be thought of as dangers), then you will probably start to feel nervous each time you think about the presentation. This is normal. Everybody, including well-trained professional speakers, feels a little scared sometimes before they speak. However, if the fear makes you put the presentation off until the last minute, skip school the day the presentation is due, or causes you to ignore your other schoolwork, that is **not** normal. Instead, it is excessive.

Actually, it is the fear of what you <u>think</u> will happen, **not** the actual event, that makes you scared or nervous. The thoughts you have about a situation are known as the *perception* of the situation. The *perception* of the situation includes the amount of danger you assign to that situation; it is also what causes some of the fear and nervousness you experience in some situations. Sometimes, your *perception* of a situation may lead you to believe something is scary. Consider this example. You get into a small plane operated by someone you just met. You are belted into the plane and taken up several hundred feet into the air. Then, the plane is turned facing almost straight down, and you fall toward the earth below. If you were forced to do this, your *perception* of the situation would most likely be one of danger, which would also cause you some feelings of fear and nervousness. Now consider a similar situation. Suppose you decide to ride the tallest, fastest roller coaster in the world. If you really like roller coasters, then you would probably not have a *perception* of danger, but rather would have a *perception* of fun. In the examples, similar situations produce very different *perceptions*: one involved danger, which caused fear and nervousness, while the other did not involve danger, and no fear was experienced. In order to understand your fear of taking tests, it is important to realize your *perception* of tests is what causes that feeling, **not** the test itself. Once you learn tests do not present any danger to you, your fear of taking them will be reduced.

Can a Small Amount of Fear Be Good?

Becoming fearful when faced with challenges or important situations is not only normal, it can be a good thing. Why? Because the same fear that makes us ready to run or fight is also the feeling that gets us motivated to do our best. When soccer players get ready to kick free kicks in the box with only 20 seconds left, they must have enough motivation to do their best. If they let themselves become distracted by fear, they might "choke." To deal with the fear the situation presents, thoughts turn to the kick and the goal, some deep breaths are taken, and concentration on the shot is used to turn the fear into something useful: motivation.

Taking the WASL may cause you some concern. You may worry about doing well or finishing the test in a reasonable amount of time. Instead of letting your fears get the best of you, you should take those feelings and use them to motivate yourself to do your best, just as you would use your fears to motivate yourself before taking a free kick. If you feel a little scared, say to yourself, "This is OK. It's normal. In fact, it's helpful." When you say these things, you are thinking of the fear as normal and accepting it. It seems strange to some students that accepting fear actually makes them less nervous. For most students, that is exactly what happens.

Exercise #1: Being Scared and Being Motivated

Fill out the chart below.

⇨ Practice thinking that being a little frightened is OK.

⇨ List the times when being a little scared got you motivated.

Not Psyched   Very Psyched

0   2   4   6   8   10

Not Scared   Extremely Scared

List of Times When Being a Little Scared Got Me Motivated		
Describe Situations In Which You Became Scared	**How Scared You Were (Rate 0 to 10)**	**How Motivated You Were (Rate 0 to 10)**

What Is Test Anxiety?

Anxiety is a fancy word for being afraid or nervous about something. The feelings of fear and nervousness you experience about tests are known as test anxiety and are a combination of at least three different things. First, you can <u>feel</u> anxiety in your body, so anxiety is physical. Second, you can <u>see</u> anxiety in what you do, so anxiety causes actions. Third, you can <u>hear</u> anxiety in the things you say to yourself, so anxiety causes certain thoughts.

How Your Body Feels When You Are Nervous

You usually know you are nervous if your body feels scared. You might start to think about being scared before your body tells you you're afraid, but in the end, it is almost always your body that reacts to whatever you perceive as a danger. According to psychologists, fear is usually felt in our bodies in such ways as increased heartbeats, rapid breathing, sweating, tightened muscles, and/or dry mouth. Sometimes, you might pace the floor, not be able to sleep, or go to the bathroom more than usual. This is your body's normal way of getting ready for any event that it perceives as dangerous enough to scare you, so if it needs to, it can fight back or eliminate the threat. It is important to understand your body's reactions are normal and are to be expected if something makes you nervous.

Often, when you notice your body reacting this way, you begin to think about how scared you are, and it sometimes makes you even more frightened. It's as if you say to yourself, "If my body is this freaked out, then the situation must really be dangerous."

Anxiety can be felt by your body in many different ways. Below is a description of some ways different parts of your body feel when you become nervous or anxious.

heart	pounding, beating much harder than usual
breathing	very quick, sometimes hyperventilating, short of breath
muscles	very tense, feeling sore and achy
stomach	butterflies, upset, vomiting
mouth	becomes dry
vision	hard to focus, vision can be blurry
head	headaches, sometimes the feeling of a rubber band around forehead
hands, feet	numbness, tingling, shaking
throat	closes up, swallowing is hard
digestive system	constipation, diarrhea, urinating frequently

As you can see, your body reacts many different ways when you are nervous. It reacts these ways because it is a part of our genetic makeup. Since the beginning of time, humans have had to be able to fight or run away from dangerous situations that might present a life threatening situation. Over time, it became our bodies' natural reaction to react to any threatening situation by being nervous or anxious. Today, we still protect ourselves in a similar way, even if the threat, like the WASL, isn't going to physically harm us. Remember, you react to what you believe to be a threat, whether the situation really is threatening. Your body reacts the same way to an assessment test as it does to something that might be dangerous. You cannot run away from tests. You must calm yourself down, because physical reactions, like headaches or feeling sick, can get in the way of your ability to think clearly on the WASL.

What You Do When You're Nervous

When you learn to be afraid of tests, you begin to act in fairly predictable ways. You might try to avoid the thing that makes you nervous. You'll see yourself delaying your study time, watching TV, or making phone calls. When the test time arrives, you might get up late, be late for school, or, if your anxiety is really bad, you might skip school. You do something called *procrastination*, which is putting things off or avoiding things because they make you nervous. If you are an "avoider," you are letting the anxiety make you do things that will hurt your performance on the WASL.

You also might be the type of person who overreacts to the anxiety. You may study all the time, read and reread passages, underline every sentence in study material, and take a very long time to read a very short passage. When the time comes to take the WASL, you may not have studied everything because you ran out of time. You are too *perfectionistic*, believing that if you try to do everything perfectly and are extremely careful to make things perfect while taking the WASL, you will do better. Unfortunately, since you can't really be perfect, and you can't possibly remember every detail of the material you are being assessed on, you won't be helped by the perfectionism.

How You Think When You're Nervous

When students are nervous about tests, many times they begin to have more and more thoughts that make them even more anxious. These thoughts can appear very rapidly, seeming as if they are automatic ideas that come whether you want them to or not. Oftentimes, these thoughts feel so real that you forget they are just ideas, and you begin to believe your thoughts are actually true. When that happens, you begin to react emotionally to the thoughts. Your perception of the situation and the huge threat you see it as becomes as real to you as any physical threat. That is how ideas can lead to anxiety.

There are certain types of thoughts that seem to affect how we feel. Below is a list of the types of thoughts that can often lead to anxiety. When you find yourself feeling nervous about the WASL, check out your thinking to see if you are having any of these kinds of thoughts:

Useless Thoughts

Black and white thinking	thoughts that describe everything as all bad or all good
Mind reading	thinking you know what other people think about you
Catastrophizing	predicting a terrible thing will happen; making things so bad in the future they are beyond repair
Jumping to conclusions	drawing a conclusion when you don't really have enough information to reach the conclusion
Future predicting	deciding you know what will happen next without any good reason to make the prediction
Discounting	deciding that information which suggests the test is not such a threat isn't important to consider
"Should" statements	second guessing yourself by thinking that you "should" have done something else, and then only focusing on what you wish you had done instead of what you will do differently now

Beating Anxiety on the WASL

The rest of this chapter will help you handle your anxiety by giving you ways to deal with your body's reactions, your fearful actions, and your automatic thoughts. Be sure to try all the exercises. Each exercise is designed to help you learn how to handle anxiety on the WASL.

Beating Perfectionism

One anxiety problem that is tough to overcome is *perfectionism*. *Perfectionism* is trying too hard to make a situation perfect. All your thoughts and energy are focused on making things exactly right, rather than concentrating on the task at hand. Most students who become perfectionistic don't see their ideas about the test or their overreactive strategies as problems. Their ideas seem reasonable because, to a certain degree, they are; making sure you do things right is OK to a certain degree. When students' perfectionistic ideas grow into an overreaction, they begin to lose time thinking about what they must do next, studying insignificant material too long, and spending their time inefficiently.

Examining Your Perfectionism

The first step to overcoming *perfectionism* is to see if you have a problem. Check yourself out. If you spend more than an hour worrying about the WASL or do repetitive actions, such as underlining every sentence or repeatedly rereading the same page, you might be a perfectionist. Also, if you find the stress you feel when you think about the WASL is fairly great, or if you feel lots of stress when you're not able to perform actions you think are routine, you are probably experiencing *perfectionism*. Complete Exercise #2 to get an idea of your degree of *perfectionism*.

Exercise #2: Examining My Perfectionism

⇨ Fill in the chart below using the scale to rate your stress. Answer the questions that follow.

Perfectionism Exercise	
Hours Spent in Test Perfectionism	**Hours**
1. hours spent in thought about tests per day	
2. hours spent doing repetitive study habits per day	
Total hours for 1 and 2	
Stress from Test Perfectionism	**Stress Level**
3. stress you feel when thinking about a test (use scale above)	
4. stress felt if you don't do the repetitive habits (use scale above)	
Total Stress Level	

Is it more than one hour when you add up rows 1 & 2?   yes _____ no _____

Is the stress in row 3 or 4 a rating of 3 or greater?   yes _____ no _____

If you answered yes to both questions, you are probably experiencing perfectionism.

Challenging Your Perfectionistic Thoughts

The next step is to correct the perceptions of danger or threat that are being caused by your *perfectionism*. Of course, this is not easily done when you are already nervous, so the first thing you want to consider is reducing the stress you feel. This can be done through a process called *habituation*.

Habituation is a complex name for getting bored with something that used to get you excited or anxious. Take a moment and think about the feeling of having your shoe on your foot. Before you were asked to do that, you probably didn't feel your shoe today except for when you put it on earlier. Your body is habituated or used to the sensations from your shoe, producing a sort of "boredom" that led your body to be "unexcited" by the shoe. Your body habituated to the shoe because it does not have a *perception* the shoe presents any danger. The same thing can be done about anxious thoughts related to perfectionism.

Take some time right now to write down, on cards or a piece of paper, your anxious, perfectionistic thoughts. When you have time, set aside about an hour, and think about those ideas over and over again, making the thoughts as real as you can by picturing them in your head. Concentrate as hard as you can for the whole hour. At first, your anxiety will climb, since you aren't doing a perfectionistic activity to reduce it, but after a while, and certainly by the end of the hour, you'll notice the stress from the thoughts has dropped considerably. If you keep doing this every day, after a while, you'll probably notice much less anxiety from the thoughts throughout the whole hour. If this works for you, whenever those thoughts come, tell yourself they are normal and there is no need to worry; you know how to handle them.

Breaking Your Perfectionistic Habits

When you try to break these habits, you'll find it very difficult. So, if you slip back into them from time to time, don't give up, keep going. After lots of practice, you'll break them for the most part.

The first thing to do is write down your habits, one by one. This is a good time to find a couple of other students and ask them if they notice your *perfectionism*, and get their observations of your habits, too. Once you know what your perfectionistic habits (such as rereading, excessive underlining or note taking) are, figure out when you do them. Sometimes, students only do them when preparing for a test or maybe only in certain classes. Once you've figured out what you do and when you do it, prepare to do an experiment. Set aside a week when you don't do the habit, and you'll be very careful to keep from doing it when you usually do. Ask people, such as friends, relatives, or teachers, to help you notice when you are being perfectionistic. By preventing your perfectionistic habits for that long, you will initially become stressed, but after a while, you should become less stressed as you notice nothing bad happening.

Keeping Your Body from Fighting Against You

When your body becomes nervous or anxious while you are studying for the WASL, or when you are actually taking it, you need to relax your body. There are two ways to do this: learning to calm down the body itself and stopping yourself from paying too much attention to your body.

Calming Your Body

You are about to learn how to relax your body in three ways: focused breathing, focused attention, and muscle relaxation. Even though all three ways are useful, you may find one is better for you than the others. If so, use that method to relax, and don't waste your time on the other ones. The most important thing about relaxing is finding a method that works for you. You should practice relaxing every day.

1. **You will learn how to focus on your breathing.** You might remember one of the things that happens when your body reacts to anxiety is that you breath rapidly. You can use your breathing to control the anxiety. Read these instructions, and then follow them.

   Sit back in a soft chair, put a pillow behind your head to support your neck, and then close your eyes. While your eyes are closed, begin to breath slowly in a steady rhythm. Now, begin to pay attention to your breath as it comes in. Notice how cool it feels inside your nostrils. Notice, too, how the breath is warm as it passes out. Say to yourself, "Cool air in, warm air out, RELAX." Do that for about two minutes. Once that is done, begin to focus on the feeling of your chest expanding when you breathe in and contracting when you breathe out. Say to yourself, "Expand, contract, RELAX." Do that for about two minutes. Once you're done, rate yourself on Test Anxiety Exercise #3 on the next page to describe how relaxed you became from the focused breathing.

2. **You will learn how to focus your attention.** Sit back in your chair with a pillow to support your neck. Now, begin to concentrate as much as you can on something or somewhere you like. Some people use images of the beach or a cool pond. For example, while relaxing, try to see yourself on the beach, feeling the hot sun on your skin and smelling the tanning oils from others around you. Make the image as real as you can — that will allow you to concentrate while you relax. Other people say the same word over and over again or they recite poetry, while others work out complex problems, such as reciting multiplication tables to themselves. Whatever you do, make sure the idea helps you concentrate as much as you can while trying to relax. Do the concentration exercise for about ten minutes, and then rate yourself on Test Anxiety Exercise #3 on the next page to describe how relaxed you became from focusing your attention.

3. **You will learn how to relax your muscles.** Sit back in your chair with your neck supported by a pillow. Now, begin to focus on the following muscles, one at a time, for about 30 seconds each, and keep saying to yourself the word "RELAX." While you focus on each muscle area, allow the tension in those muscles to drain out and allow the muscles to become heavy and warm. They should feel like they are drooping. Try this order: feet, lower legs, upper legs, stomach, chest, lower back, upper back, shoulders, upper arms, lower arms, hands, neck, jaw, face, eyes, forehead. As with the other exercises, rate yourself on Test Anxiety Exercise Sheet #3 on the next page to describe how relaxed you became from your attempts to relax your muscles.

4. Once you've learned to relax, begin your relaxation exercises by taking a deep breath, holding it for five to ten seconds, saying to yourself, "RELAX," and then letting your body relax. This will create a "signal breath," or a cue to help your body relax later. After the "signal breath," you should use the relaxing strategies that work for you.

When you are taking the WASL, you may not be able to do the focused breathing, the focused attention, or the muscle relaxation, so it is important to have a cue to bring on some relaxation. By using a "signal breath," you are teaching your body to relax in response to the breath. You can use the "signal breath" during the WASL if you find your body becoming anxious. Now, practice using a signal breath followed by the relaxation strategies you feel work best for you and record your exercises just as you did with the other three methods for relaxing on Test Anxiety Exercise #3.

Most importantly, if you find relaxation strategies that work, practice your relaxation exercises every day.

Exercise #3: Relaxation
⇨ Rate how anxious you are using a scale where 0 = extremely relaxed and 100 = extremely anxious. Also, note how well you concentrated.

Strategy	Pre-Strategy Anxiety Rating: How you feel when you're anxious (0-100)	How well you kept your mind on what you were doing (0-100)	Post-Strategy Anxiety Rating: How you feel after the exercise (0-100)
1. Breathing exercise to relax			
2. Focusing – relaxing while you concentrate			
3. Muscle Relaxation – getting rid of tension			
4. Signal Breathing			

Paying Less Attention To Your Body
Some students have developed a keen sense of what their bodies are doing from one minute to the next. When they become anxious, they begin to notice the early physical signs, such as a headache, sweating, or soreness in their muscles. By paying so much attention to their bodies, they are distracted from doing their best on the WASL.

These students also begin to get nervous about what their bodies are doing, and then they get even more anxious from overattending to their bodies. If you find you pay so much attention to your body that you become anxious because you worry about what your body might do, then you may want to learn how to distract your attention from your body.

First, try shifting your attention to something more important, like the material in the Mathematics chapter of this book. If that doesn't work, try something called *Thought Stopping*. When you notice you are paying too much attention to your body, smack a book or your hand on a table (not too hard, you wouldn't want to break the table or your hand) and say, at the same time, "STOP." The loud noise and the word stop should interfere with your attention to your body. If it works, then practice just saying the word "STOP" out loud for a few times, and then say it just in your head. Saying the word "STOP" in your head usually can help you bring an end to the attention you are paying to your body.

Controlling Your Anxious Actions

Avoiding the Situation

Sometimes, acting scared is almost automatic. You don't even seem to think about the thing making you scared; it just seems to have a power of its own. For example, when you touched something hot, you learned that it really hurt. You learned to avoid things that are hot because there is a possible danger associated with hot objects. Some young children who were mildly burned by hot water will go through some very scary nights of taking baths before they learn that not all water is going to burn them. Before they learn that lesson, they get REALLY SCARED. It's the same with assessment tests. Ever since you've been a student in school, the importance of testing has been very clear. For some people, bad experiences with tests have made them nervous or scared about all tests. Maybe their friends made fun of them for doing poorly, or maybe people important to them got mad at them when they didn't do as well as those people thought they should. Perhaps they studied hard in a particular class and found it didn't matter, they still didn't do well on the test. Experiences like these make you think tests are scary. It's not a lot different than the "hot-water fear." Just as the young child probably tried to stay away from the water in the tub after he or she were burned, you learned to avoid tests after you were "burned" by an exam or quiz.

Familiarize Yourself with the Situation

One really effective way of learning not to be scared in situations like these is to expose yourself over and over again to the frightening thing (in this case, the WASL) a little bit at a time. Each time, make the "little bit" bigger, until you are facing the whole thing. This process is called *familiarization*. By exposing yourself to what you fear again and again, you will begin to become familiar with what it is you fear, and that thing will not be so unfamiliar and scary to you anymore.

Let's apply this idea to the WASL. The things you need to be familiar with on the WASL are 1) the material, 2) the questions and 3) the actual experience of taking the assessment. One way to learn to be less anxious is to practice taking test questions, a few at first, but eventually practicing whole sets of forty or fifty. Another way to reduce your fears is to become familiar with the actual experience of taking the WASL. Some of this is accomplished by practicing test questions, but there is another part: the test-taking situation. You will be taking the WASL at school. If you study and practice test questions in a similar environment, you will be exposed to surroundings that are much like the actual experience of taking the WASL. As the newness of this situation wears off, so will the fear that is associated with taking the WASL. By getting used to whatever it is that makes you nervous or anxious, you will begin to turn your fears into motivation to succeed.

Exercise #4: Familiarization Plan
- ⇨ Fill out the chart below.
- ⇨ Develop a plan for familiarizing yourself with the WASL.

Test Anxiety Familiarization Program for the WASL

In the chart below, design your own plan for increasing your familiarity with the WASL. Be sure to follow this plan in order to have the best chance of doing your best on the WASL. Indicate the number of practice items and the test they are from – Listening, Reading, Writing, or Mathematics – under the Test Subject column. Indicate the place and date where you studied for each subject. When you are finished with the practice items, write your initials under the Initials/Verification column. Try to increase the number of practice items you do for each session.

	Place	Date	Test Subject	Initials/Verification
Session 1			Test Subject: _____ # of items: _____	
Session 2			Test Subject: _____ # of items: _____	
Session 3			Test Subject: _____ # of items: _____	
Session 4			Test Subject: _____ # of items: _____	

Decrease Your Anxious Actions: Break the Anxiety-Avoidance Cycle
If you believe that you know very little, whether this is true or not, you will likely be scared. If you are scared enough, you will deny being scared and act like the test is not a big deal. This happens because of the anxiety-avoidance cycle.

Here's how it works. The more nervous or anxious you are about the WASL, the more you try to avoid it; the less anxious you are, the more prepared you feel. Anxiety and your avoidance of the WASL are interdependent, meaning as one goes up, so does the other.

The anxiety you have about the WASL not only increases your avoidance of the assessment, it also decreases the amount of time and energy you have to prepare for and think clearly about the WASL. As your energy level goes down, you begin to feel more frightened. You begin to believe you are all alone and there is no way out. You then begin to believe you will do very poorly on the WASL, and also begin to think you are a poor student. High anxiety causes more avoidance of, and less opportunity for, success on the WASL.

As your anxiety grows and your ability to think clearly decreases, you start to believe there are other reasons for not doing well on the WASL. Maybe it's the school's fault. Maybe, if you are not studying, then it's because, "I couldn't study," not because, "I didn't want to study." Your mind starts to ignore any "evidence" that you can succeed; it only sees reasons why you can't succeed and puts a "wall" around your beliefs, only letting things in that will be sure to support your beliefs that you can't do well. Not doing your best on the WASL may mean you decided not to succeed, although you will try to give yourself a reason to say you couldn't succeed. If you don't prepare for the WASL, you are trying to create an excuse for not doing well, but the reality is that you avoided studying.

At some point, you realize your avoidance is wrong, but now all that time has passed. With too little time to study, you begin to panic more, so the fear level goes up and the cycle begins all over again. As long as you perceive the material covered on the test is a danger to you, you will be plagued by this cycle. The key to breaking this cycle is to reduce your anxiety using the methods described in this chapter. By doing this, you will be less likely to try to avoid the test and less likely to spend your time looking for excuses about why you will perform poorly. Also, by reducing anxiety, you will provide yourself with a better opportunity to do your best because your energy will be focused on how to succeed on the WASL instead of how to avoid it. As your mastery of the WASL increases, your anxiety will decrease.

One method you may want to use to do this is to break down the materials to be studied into smaller parts and identify each one as a unique body of information. For the WASL, the topics you need to study can be seen in the material provided to you in the rest of this book.

Changing Your Anxious Ideas

Developing a Positive Attitude
There are many ways to convince ourselves the WASL is the worst thing that will happen to us during school. This is not true, but during the time before the test, it is easily believed. Below are some common ideas about the WASL that are not true but easy to think. You'll recall these Useless Thoughts from page 5:

✓ I am the only one scared of the WASL. [*Black and White Thinking*]

✓ My mother and father will be so disappointed in me if I do poorly. [*Mind Reading*]

✓ The test is too hard. [*Black and White Thinking*]

✓ If I do poorly, my life is ruined. [*Catastrophizing*]

✓ If I am this scared now, I'll never get the answers right. [*Jumping to Conclusions*]

✓ The school didn't get me ready, so I probably will do poorly. [*Future Predicting*]

✓ My teacher is really expecting me to do well, so if I don't, he (she) won't like me anymore. [*Mind Reading*]

✓ The test isn't really important. They'll probably get rid of it before I take it anyway. Nobody else takes it seriously either. [*Discounting*]

✓ I can always take it again later, so why try this time. I'll just practice on this one. [*Discounting*]

Now let's think of some other ways to think about the test that you can use to replace the Useless Thoughts. You can do this pretty easily by using ideas from past experiences. For example, if you think you are the only one who is upset about the test, you might think about how many of your classmates have talked about their nervous feelings just before taking a test. You've probably even talked with some of your friends about the WASL and found out they are "uptight" about the test as well. Try to think of replacement thoughts to substitute for the Useless Thoughts listed on the previous page.

Exercise #5: Useless Thoughts

⇨ Look at the chart below. On your own piece of paper, write a replacement thought that proves why the Useless Thought is incorrect.

Getting Rid of Useless Thoughts
Useless Thought
I am the only one scared of the WASL.
My mother and father will be so disappointed in me if I do poorly.
The WASL is too hard.
If I do poorly, my life is ruined.
If I am this scared now, I'll never get the answers right.
The school didn't get me ready, so I probably will do poorly.
My teacher expects me to do well, so if I don't, he (she) won't like me anymore.

Show What You Know®

The fact that you are taking the WASL should tell you that you are bright enough to be a seventh grader in your school. Of course, you may have forgotten some of the information you'll need for the WASL, but you can study, review, or relearn that material. The bottom line is you have passed the "entrance" requirement for the WASL: you have been promoted to the seventh grade.

If that is true, then you must change your thinking to believe the WASL is a great chance for you to show what you know®. On a test like the WASL, even knowing some of the answers are wrong counts if you can use that knowledge to get closer to the right answer. So, you should start believing you are a good student, you are able to relearn whatever you have forgotten, and you are capable of showing all that you know because the Commission of Student Learning in Washington has provided you with an opportunity to prove how much you have learned. You can call that opportunity the WASL.

Exercise #6: Show What You Know®

➯ Make a list of reasons you would tell others to show you are qualified to take the WASL. Use the heading given below to get started.

A List Of Reasons Why I'm Qualified To Take the WASL
1.
2.
3.
4.
5.

You Are Not the WASL

Many of the scary thoughts you have about the WASL come from a belief that how you do on the test is a statement about you as an individual. This is not true. This test is just an assessment you must complete to continue your education. You have to take classes, such as math, science, history, and English, too. You have to pass the tests in these classes to complete school. The WASL is just another hurdle you must jump in order to get to the finish line. How you do on it tells you <u>nothing</u> about you as a person. It only tells you how well you can apply knowledge in this testing situation. So, while doing well on the WASL is important, you are still the same great person you were before the assessment, no matter how you do on it.

Exercise #7: You Are Not the WASL

➯ On your own piece of paper, make a list of things you know about the WASL. Then, make a list that describes you. Write down all the ways you are different from the WASL. Think about how you are not the same as what your score will be on the WASL. Use the heading given below.

The "I am not the WASL" Comparison Sheet		
Description of the WASL	Description of Me	How I am Different from My Score on the WASL

You Are the One Taking the WASL

It is very tempting for teachers and parents to judge how well <u>they</u> have done their jobs by how well <u>you</u> do in your life. This is normal. However, sometimes parents and teachers can get stressed by events that you are going through as if they are going through the events themselves. When this happens, it is also easy for you to get nervous. Most of you have thought, "If my teacher (or parent) is so 'freaked out' by the WASL, it must be really awful. I guess I should be scared too." DON'T BE! You are taking the WASL, not your teachers or parents. While parents and teachers may feel like they are being judged by how well you do on the WASL, remind them the test is about you and your education. It's good you care about how they feel, but remember, you are taking the WASL, so your feelings are most important while preparing and taking the test.

Exercise #8: Imagine You Are Not Scared

⇨ Close your eyes and try to imagine a crowd of people including yourself, your parents, and your teachers. See them all frightened. Now see yourself not scared, walking out of the crowd. Try it right now!

The WASL Is Real, But It Is Only an Assessment

Some people may say the WASL is not really important. Some will say it doesn't matter; others might say it will go away. A word that often is used in describing this attitude is *denial*. We deny that the WASL is important. After all, if it isn't important, then we don't have to be scared of it. If it isn't important, we don't have to do well or try hard. Just saying these things should give you a clue about how destructive such thinking can be. It takes away the healthy part of the fear that motivates you to do well. It also sets you up to perform poorly. Instead of thinking this way, see the test for what it is. The WASL is an important assessment, but it is <u>only</u> an assessment. It is necessary to take it, and it will not go away.

Exercise #9: Test Importance

⇨ Make a list of things people could say to try to convince you that the WASL is not important. Then list out reasons why it is. Use the headings given below.

Five Reasons Why the WASL Is Important to Me	
Why others say the WASL is not important.	Why the WASL is important to me.
1.	
2.	
3.	
4.	
5.	

Take the Seventh Grade WASL Just Once in Your Life

Have you ever seen a tennis match? The players try to win every point. They have to, because by the end of the match, they won't win if they don't have enough points. That is the way you should think about the WASL; make every question count. You should think about two things:

1. You can do well on the WASL once you have mastered the knowledge and test-taking problem-solving skills required, and

2. You will face the WASL this year, whether you want to or not.

The WASL is neither a danger nor a threat, but just another challenge in your academic career as a student. You will be required to take it, even if you pretend it isn't important.

Creating a Study Plan

Once you have organized the areas to be studied, set up a plan for studying.

A number of studies have been done to improve a student's studying. You can use this information to become a better test taker. Dr. George Allen, in 1970, did a study that is used to explain how to study better.

First, define what you need to study. On the WASL, there is a specific goal: do well on each section at the level set by the Commission of Student Learning in Washington. The goal is not to get all items correct or to be the first student to complete the assessment. Your goal should be to do your best on the WASL. To do that, you must know certain information that is summarized in this book. That doesn't mean other information isn't important, but for the WASL, the objective is to know the material and use it. So, first you must establish the objective: succeed on each section by knowing the material the state says you'll have to know.

Second, you must define studying, not as how much time you spend, but how well and efficiently you study. Dr. Allen tells us a study done at the University of Illinois determined that the time spent studying didn't really predict how well somebody did on a test. The first step in studying effectively is scheduling your time. You must set up a schedule every day, for the whole day, and then schedule study time as a part of the day. Take the time every day to practice with the material in this book and your school subjects, but not all at once. Make a short- and a long-term plan, deciding what you will study each day in an intensive way and what you will begin to review for basic content. Make a plan when each subject on the WASL will be covered, first in a basic way to familiarize yourself with types of questions and material, and more in-depth later.

If you notice you study better for some subjects or during certain parts of the day, take notes on your study habits for a few days. Learn to become familiar with the way you study each subject on the test. If you find that some subjects put you to sleep or lead you to avoid them, change when you study, how you study, and the amount you study to control your reactions.

Regarding the schedule: Above all, make the commitment to live by it as best you can and change those things that don't work. If you don't make the decision within yourself, the schedule will be nothing more than words on a piece of paper.

Reward yourself. You must be aware of the fact that things you find rewarding or pleasurable will influence how you spend your time. So, if studying is never very rewarding, then you are very unlikely to stick to a study schedule. Therefore, you must create a way of rewarding yourself each time you study. Some ways of doing this may be to treat yourself to a snack once you finish doing a certain number of reading questions, or setting up your study schedule so that when you finish studying, your favorite television show will be on.

Control the influences of the world around you when studying. To control the things that influence your studying, it is a good idea to follow Dr. Allen's methods:

1. Set aside time every day to study.
2. Study during the day.
3. Reward yourself with doing something you enjoy, but only if you stick to your study plan first.
4. Study alone.
5. Study only one subject at a time, and preferably for at least an hour continuously.
6. Begin to study well in advance of the test.
7. Exercise physically at least a few hours each week.
8. Arrange your study place to make it easiest for you to study effectively.

Remember, following these steps should help you decrease your study time and lead to better scores.

Sometimes, students need to change their study habits over time. To overcome old habits, one of the first things to do is to be strict with your schedule, building in routines that you follow each day, including when you study and when you don't. Each week you study, keep to the same schedule until you control your habits instead of your habits controlling you; then you will begin to be more flexible.

Now would be a good time for you to figure out things that affect your studying. Try to list the things that help you study, that you find rewarding, and that you must do each day. Create your routine and schedule the studying as described above. Then, give yourself a reward after studying. When you create your plan, stick to it.

Remember, try to study in a place like the one where you'll be taking the WASL. For example, go to the library, find a quiet study section, and sit where other people are working. Decide to use specific techniques for hard to remember ideas. A good strategy is to use colored index cards. If, for example, you find that you keep missing certain practice questions in Mathematics and Reading, use blue cards for Mathematics and white ones for Reading. Put the study material on the cards and use them as flash cards. Remember, a great way to use the cards is to write questions about the hard material on the front of the cards and put the answers on the back. That way, you are learning the material as answers to questions, which is the way you will need to know it on the WASL. As you learn the material better, you'll see the number of cards in your deck get smaller. The smaller the deck of cards, the more you know, and the less you have to be nervous about.

After you have developed your study schedule, talk with your family and teachers. Ask them to help you with questions you have when you're studying, and let them know you will be using your schedule to help you study. Ask your family to consider the importance of your studying when planning family activities. For you, preparing for the WASL is a job, and you don't want to miss work.

Exercise #10: Study Schedule

⇨   On your own piece of paper, write a letter to your family explaining your need to study when you've scheduled yourself to study, and tell them you'll need to concentrate during those times. Be sure to include the information listed below.

Study Schedule Letter Information

Be sure to include:
- what you are studying for
- when you will be studying
- why you need their help
- some specific things they can help you with (for example, helping you with your chores)
- any other information you think they need to know

Studying the Material Effectively

The method for studying recommended in research on test anxiety is called the **SQ3R**, based on work done by a psychologist from The Ohio State University named Francis Pleasant Robinson. Dr. Allen's advice is to follow the **SQ3R** method.

SQ3R Method:

1. **S**can the material so you can understand the basic idea of it and what things it includes. Read the headings and the summaries. Make a list of the major points from what you have read.

2. **Q**uestions should be created from the major headings or components in each section. Create a study diary and write out each of the newly-formed questions. Use the questions to see what you do and do not know. By knowing your strengths and weaknesses, you'll be able to use your time better. Try to create questions that either ask for definitions or facts, similarities or differences, or apply the information to problems (for example, by giving examples of how the information might work in the real world).

3. **R**ead and mark the material to sort it for its helpfulness in answering the questions you wrote down. Dr. Allen suggests using the following marks to help you sort your material:

   - **VI** (for Very Important)
   - **I** (for Important)
   - **S** (for Summary of Information)

Write these marks in the margins of the book. Also, as you read the material, take your study diary and write out the answers to questions to use for studying. While you may be used to highlighting and underlining in the book, it really doesn't help when you are studying. Use the study diary and marks instead.

As you study the notes you've taken, let your mind create pathways to the details of the information. At first, study all the material in your diary and the marked information, but begin to work backwards to the main points. Learn the details as a part of the main points so that when you try to remember something, you just go to that information in your mind, and let your mind pull out the folder with the details. You probably already do this, but don't know it. For example, when you memorize a song on the radio, at first you probably try to learn all the words, but then a couple of months later, when you hear it on the radio, all you need is the first line of the chorus, and you have the rest of it. The first line serves as a cue to the other information. So, when you study, work toward using the main points as cues. You will spend less time studying things you already know and will instead use your time wisely to memorize the important information in such a way that your brain will work efficiently.

Also, when you study, Dr. Allen's research indicates you might want to pay more attention to certain things. Remember, the goal is to learn the information that is important to the WASL. There are several types of organizing strategies in textbooks that help to find the important information.

A. Look for the topic sentence of each paragraph, which is often the first sentence.
B. Visual aides in the text such as graphs, charts, tables, often serve to summarize the important information.
C. Seek out key phrases that begin with indicator words such as "first," "second," or "to summarize." Look for indicator words that tell you the author is spending time explaining the key information.

4. Recite the information over and over again in response to the questions. Dr. Allen suggests you see the questions you've formed as an example of what will be on the WASL. If you learn the material in response to your questions, you'll be learning it in the context of how you'll be asked to remember it on the WASL itself. Do the recitation of the material you're studying out loud, repeatedly, until you know it like the back of your hand. Then, go back later in the week or month and review everything again, reciting it out loud in response to the questions. This is a strategy known as over learning, and it will make recalling facts for the WASL much easier.

5. Review what you've learned immediately after you recite, but only take a few minutes. Dr. Allen suggests the time spent on the review should be no more than five minutes. Also, every day, you should review all the material learned earlier in the day to keep it fresh. Again, be brief, but if you find you can't remember something during the review, go back to relearn it.

Summary

There are three things that affect test anxiety, and ultimately, test success. The first is **test-taking skills**. This will be reviewed in the next chapter. Second is **confidence**, which is the sense of being secure in how much you know by the seventh grade. Activities for building confidence and beating anxiety have been discussed in this chapter. The third is **knowledge**, which comes from everything you have learned by the time you are promoted to the seventh grade and from studying the required material. If you refine your test-taking skills, reduce your test anxiety, and know the material, you can do well on the WASL. In the diagram below, the shaded area represents the combination of the three ingredients that will result in your ultimate goal: success on the WASL!

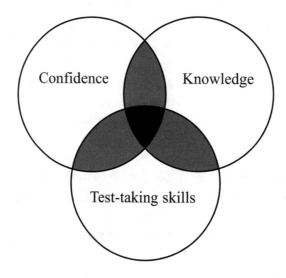

Test-Taking Strategies

Test-Taking Skills for the WASL

Knowing your Opponent

Experts tell us one thing that makes students scared about tests is they don't know enough about them. The same is true about the Washington Assessment of Student Learning (WASL): it seems too big and fuzzy. Of course, the WASL is not really your opponent; it is just an assessment, but maybe if we think of it as an opponent for now, it will help you to understand the idea that you must know enough about the WASL to do well on it. In the previous chapter, this idea is referred to as *familiarization*.

What's on the WASL and how does it work?

The first thing to know is what the Commission of Student Learning in Washington wants you to be able to know, and how to use what you know to solve problems and answer questions. There are different things you need to know and be able to do by seventh grade on each of four separate assessments on the WASL: Listening, Reading, Writing, and Mathematics. The chapters later in the book will review this information.

The test-taking and problem-solving strategies taught in this book are designed specifically to deal with the WASL. Specially selected teachers wrote the chapters on Listening, Reading, Writing, and Mathematics for this book. This team of teachers was able to use their knowledge to help you study and understand WASL questions as if you too were an expert on the WASL. You should feel like one when you are finished with this book!

The test-taking strategies in this book will show you how to:
1. figure out the multiple-choice answers that look right, but are wrong,
2. use all the knowledge you have to be the best guesser you can be, if you have to guess,
3. perform well on short-answer and extended-response questions, and
4. be confident and calm when you take the WASL so you can do your best.

It is very important to understand that taking a test is something you learn to do. When you were in elementary school, the tests you took in first and second grade were pretty simple. One of the reasons you took any kind of tests when you were that young was to teach you how to take a test. It's like learning the words to a new song on a CD. First you practice a few times, and after you sing it over and over, you can remember the words without even thinking about them. You learn how to sing the song. Taking the WASL is just like learning a song, but in this case, you don't really know the "words" yet. To prepare yourself for the WASL, you will need to practice. Also, since you won't know exactly what is on the WASL until you take it, it is important to be prepared by learning how to make any test taking experience successful.

To help you learn how to take a test, we will teach you test-taking skills by going over them, so you understand what they are, and then help you learn all the important information that may appear on the WASL. Finally, we will teach you how to apply the information on practice test questions that are very much like the ones you'll see on the WASL. When you solve these practice questions, we will show you how to use test-taking skills to apply what you know. We teach you how to get the most credit for your knowledge and to use the WASL as an opportunity to show what you know®.

To learn how to take the WASL, you must think like a WASL author. The people who wrote the questions on the WASL had to follow certain rules so their questions were picked for the test. They had to write questions that were fair, so the test isn't too hard. Remember, the WASL was not written to trick you, but to give you the best chance to succeed.

Another important thing to remember is that this book is not going to replace what you learned in school. The schools have done a good job teaching you Listening, Reading, Writing, and Mathematics. This book goes over information you already learned in school and shows you which information is most important on the WASL. Most importantly, though, is what this book teaches you about taking tests. There are three very important ingredients to doing well on a test or an assessment: **knowledge**, **test-taking skills**, **and confidence**. This book will teach you all three; this chapter will teach you test-taking skills.

We want you to learn to use your knowledge to find wrong answers and rule them out. This helps you find the right answers.

We want you to learn how to analyze the questions so you figure out the problem the writers of the WASL are asking you to solve.

We want you to learn what types of short-answer and extended-response questions to expect.

Get ready to learn test-taking skills!

Multiple-Choice Questions

You deserve to get credit for what you do know, even if you don't know the right answer to a multiple-choice question. That probably sounds a little strange, but take a moment to think about it. If you know some of the answers can't be right, you rule those out. At least you know wrong answers are wrong. If you have only one or two answers left, you have a pretty good chance of getting the question right, even if you still don't know the right answer. You get credit for the part of your knowledge that relates to the wrong answers.

When you guess, guess wisely. If you read a question and don't know the information, you should go over the answers to see if you know something about them. Rule out some of the answers, and when you have two or three left, you can guess wisely — use the power of knowing that you have a better chance of getting the question right now than before. **Never leave a question blank**. Use your guessing power to give yourself the chance to earn the most points you possibly can.

Ruling out wrong answers is important to answering multiple-choice items. Finding out which answer is right is often a process of deciding which answers are wrong. By ruling out some answers, you will be able to see more clearly which one is right. Below is an example of how this works.

1. Which unsuccessful former presidential candidate was once an astronaut in the 1960s?

   ○ A. Ronald Reagan
   ○ B. John Glenn
   ○ C. George W. Bush
   ○ D. Bill Clinton

   Analysis: You know it's not Ronald Reagan or Bill Clinton since they were both successfully elected President. It can't be George W. Bush, since he was recently elected in 2000. It must be John Glenn. Of course, if you remembered that John Glenn was an astronaut, you probably also could have used that to get to John Glenn. I'll bet you didn't even know he ran for president once, but somehow you got it right anyway.

You can see that by knowing something about the wrong answers, you can get the question right. You may think that guessing is wrong to do, but it's not. Getting a question wrong because you didn't use all that you know is wrong. You're not any worse off if you guess. Rule out any wrong answers and go for it — guess.

It is important to answer every question — even if you guess! You have a 1 out of 4 chance for getting a question right, even if you don't rule out any answers. That means that for every four questions you guess, you should get one question right. Now imagine that you rule out one of the answers. That makes your chances 1 out of 3. If you rule out two answers, then the odds are 1 out of 2. Each time you rule out an answer and then go ahead and guess, you keep increasing the odds that you will get more and more of the questions right, even if you guess.

You are allowed to write on the test booklet, except during the Writing section. This is the only time you'll get paper. So don't try to remember which answers you've ruled out. Instead, draw a line through the answers you rule out. Just cross them out.

Finding Distracters

When the question writers provide questions for the WASL, they are also asked to provide incorrect answers that students may easily mistake for the correct answer. For example, in the Mathematics section, the writer would provide incorrect answers using numbers he or she got from performing the math incorrectly. These incorrect answers are called "distracters" because they catch your attention and distract you from using all your knowledge to solve the problem in the question. In order to avoid choosing a distracter as an answer, you must think like a test question writer and try to imagine what kinds of distracter answers you would write. When you think like that, you can spot the distracters, and then you won't pick them so often, thus improving your score.

You see, some of the questions on the test are really "hard." Not hard because the questions ask about little known things, but hard because most students get them wrong. Sometimes, it's possible that more students miss a question when they don't guess than they would if they did guess. Why? Because on some questions, the wrong answers are written to look right. Your job is to spot these distracters and avoid picking them. This doesn't mean that every answer that looks correct is wrong! It means that you should be careful about just picking answers on hard problems without thinking through each of the answers first. The best way to avoid choosing distracters is to answer the question twice to be sure the information and method you used were correct.

Analyzing the Answers

Why are all those answers there on the multiple-choice questions? There is a reason. Many of the test answers on the WASL are there because they represent answers that are common mistakes easily made by students when calculating an answer. These answers look right because they are so easy to come to, but they are really wrong. Consider this sample item.

2. You receive an allowance of $5.00 per week. If you do the laundry, you earn an extra $5.00 per week. If you cut the grass, you get an extra $3.00 per week. When you took care of your younger brother after school, you earned $12.00 for four hours of baby-sitting. Last week you baby-sat four hours. How much extra money can you earn if you cut the grass and baby-sit two hours next week?

   ○ A. $8.00
   ○ B. $9.00
   ○ C. $15.00
   ○ D. $27.00

   Analysis: Answer D is the answer you would get if you tried to solve the problem and didn't read the whole question carefully. You might confuse the amount you earned for 4 hours as the amount you earned per hour. If you did make that mistake, you would have multiplied 2 x 12, arriving at 24. Then adding 24 + 3 would have produced 27, which is Answer D. The wrong answers are often there because they represent easy-to-make mistakes. Answer B is correct.

It is comforting to see the answer you came up with printed on the page. You immediately think, "It must be right, my answer is there on the page." Many of the wrong answers on the WASL are selected so that if you make a common mistake, you'll get an answer that will be on the page. The lesson to learn is to use the techniques found in this book and something called "rating the answers."

Rating the Answers

Step 1: Read all the answer choices.

Step 2: Rate each one with a +, /, or –.

Sometimes, one answer can be better than other answers, but all might seem a little bit right. This often happens when the questions are about a reading passage or an historical document. To use the rating system, mark a "+" by answer choices that your pretty sure are correct; put a "/" by answers you're not sure about; and put a "–" by answer choices you know are wrong. Be sure to decide why you rated some answers low before answering the question. If you have only one "+" answer, mark that one. If you have more than one "+" answer, rethink what you've done because two answers can't be right. Then, guess which is best, mark it, and move on to the next question. Let's try rating the answers from the Math question on the previous page.

- A. $8.00 (No — This is the sum of either the allowance or the laundry plus cutting the grass).
+ B. $9.00 (Yes — This is the sum of three $3.00 payments: $3.00 for cutting the grass and $3.00 for each of the two hours of baby-sitting).
- C. $15.00 (No — This is the sum of what you would get for 4 hours of baby-sitting plus cutting the grass).
- D. $27.00 (No — This is the sum of 2 times $12.00 plus $3.00 for cutting the grass).

See how much easier it has become to see and choose the correct answer?

Short-Answer and Extended-Response Questions

There are a number of questions on the WASL that require you to write out a response. These are referred to as short-answer and extended-response questions.

In general, there are five basic types of short-answer and extended-response questions:
1. explaining how to apply a concept,
2. reproducing already learned information,
3. predicting what might be the logical outcome from facts,
4. identifying information provided in the question and providing that information in the answer, and
5. supporting or defending your answer.

1. Explaining How to Apply a Concept

Explaining how to apply a concept is telling how something works. On the WASL, sometimes you must be able to apply concepts to problems and tell how they work. The "tell how they work" is the extended-response part of the question. Usually, these kinds of questions will ask you to explain why something is one way or another, or it will ask you to explain how to arrive at an answer that might have already been provided. Look for "why" questions to be on the alert for this type of question.

Suppose, for example, in the Mathematics section, you are asked to explain why the area of a square should **NOT** be 33 cm². The question has to do with a square that has sides with a length of 5 cm. and an original area of 25 cm². The sides of the square are all increased in length by an additional 2 cm. You aren't just asked to calculate on the Math test, you are asked to understand Math concepts and to explain how to apply them to a question. In this example, you must know that the area of a square with a side 7 cm. in length is not 33 cm². You could explain, for example that 7 cm. times 7 cm. is 49 cm². Or you could explain that the square's new area would not be found by adding the extra 8 cm. to the original area of 25 cm². Ultimately, to answer questions like this, you must know a) the concept, b) why it applies in this case, and c) how to explain how to apply the concept. Whether it is in Mathematics or any of the other tests, you must know enough about the concepts to answer the question, so be sure to read the chapters in this book to refresh your memory of WASL concepts.

2. Reproducing Already Learned Information

There are some questions that simply require you to remember things you've learned. Of course, these questions remind you of those things, so don't forget to listen to these questions. The "already learned information" questions are fairly straightforward, often asking you to simply write something you know in an answer blank. For example, a question in the Mathematics section of the WASL may ask you to explain why scientists measure the diameter of the Earth in miles instead of inches. You could, of course, measure the diameter of the Earth in inches, but the question is asking you to address the difference between miles and inches. You must remember that a mile is considerably longer in length than an inch, and miles are used to measure larger distances. Once you remember that, you can explain that miles are used instead of inches because the use of inches would create numbers far too large to be meaningful or practical.

3. Predicting What Might Be the Logical Outcome from Facts

There are questions in the WASL that require you to use simple logic to figure out what might be the outcome of some facts. These questions ask you to reason based on past experience. There will be words in the questions like "what is the reason that. . . ." or "explain why you would. . . ." or "what did someone likely do next." All these phrases ask you either to predict the future or to explain why something that happened could have been predicted given some set of facts. This is known as making an inference. For example, you may be asked in the Reading section of the WASL to infer why Mike needed crutches. This question would be based on a reading passage. In the passage, no reasons are given, but the question and the reading sample make it pretty clear it is an inference question. Suppose the passage you read stated Mike had recently gone on a skiing trip. Although the passage may not directly state Mike broke his leg on his ski trip, you can probably infer from the passage that this is the case. Nowhere in the reading passage do you find a clear explanation of Mike's necessity of crutches, but you can infer the reason from the information provided. Ultimately, the test wants you to use your ability to infer to answer test items.

4. Identifying Information Provided in Questions and Providing that Information in Answers

Certain questions in the WASL are designed to have you reproduce things already provided in the question. These types of questions often use key words such as "identify" or "give examples from the reading" or "list from the passage." As an example, suppose you are given a passage in which you are told that William Shakespeare believed you could achieve immortality in three ways:

through writing, by having children, and through salvation. In a question following the passage, you are asked to identify three things Shakespeare considered to be means of achieving immortality. You look, find what the passage says, and list them.

So, the first part of the answer is to restate that Shakespeare believed immortality could be achieved in three ways, while the second part of the answer requires you to identify those ways, something you can obtain directly from the passage.

5. Supporting or Defending Your Answer

Some types of questions you will encounter on the WASL require you to explain why you chose the answer you did. Words that will clue you in to this are words such as "explain," "defend," or "support." For example, in the Mathematics section of the WASL, suppose you are asked to approximate the area of a square, and then explain why you chose that approximation as your answer. On the paper, the square has no marked measurements, but it looks as if each side is about 2 inches long. The approximate area is about 4 square inches. However, this is not a complete answer. To finish the question, you must explain why you arrived at that conclusion. In this case, you may say that each side is almost the same length as your thumb, which you know is a little more than 2 inches long. Then explain the math you used to find the area from that information. The most important part of defending your answer is to provide evidence, whether it be words, numbers, or pictures, that a grader will be able to understand and obtain from the information you provide.

Strategies for All Types of Questions

Analyze the Questions

Read the whole question carefully. Often, you will want to read through the question quickly, rushing to the answers to find the correct one. Sometimes, you will want to read part of a question because it is underlined or set off from the rest of the question. The WASL will probably give you some questions where formulas are set up on a reference sheet or in the middle of questions, and you may want to use the formula to solve for the correct answer.

Do Not Rush Through the Question. Read ALL of It.

Reason 1: Reading the whole question will slow you down and keep you from rushing through the test because your fear has increased.

Reason 2: Reading the whole question gives you valuable information you may need to answer the question correctly.

For example, try this problem:

3. Michael is a fourteen-year-old boy who lives in Seattle, Washington. He likes to fish, and he once caught a seven-pound salmon in the Puget Sound. He also caught a twenty-pound sturgeon in the Columbia River and a three-pound trout on a lake in Canada. The largest fish he has caught was a yellow-fin tuna in Florida. How old is Michael?

If you're like most people, you started thinking about the changing size of fish Michael had caught, believing the question had to do with the size of the fish. If you didn't read the whole problem, you'd be caught by surprise when you looked to answer the question. You'd be expecting answers about the pounds of fish, when the answers were in years of age. If you were to ignore all of the unnecessary information, your job would have been a lot simpler. In fact, take a look at the problem. If we cross out what we don't need to know, we can solve the problem.

3. Michael is a fourteen-year-old boy ~~who lives in Seattle, Washington. He likes to fish, and he once caught a seven-pound salmon in Puget Sound. He also caught a twenty-pound sturgeon in the Columbia River and a three-pound sheepshead on a lake in Canada. The largest fish he has caught was a yellow-fin tuna in Florida.~~ How old is Michael?

The answer is really obvious now isn't it? Of course this example is a little too easy to be real. But it shows that when you focus on the **real question**, the answer comes much easier.

Finding the Real Question
Now that you have read the whole question, you can figure out what the WASL is really asking. We call that the "real question." Figuring out the real question is much like other types of problem-solving methods you use every day.

Try this technique using this sample question again.

2. You receive an allowance of $5.00 per week. If you do the laundry, you earn an extra $5.00 per week. If you cut the grass, you get an extra $3.00 per week. When you took care of your younger brother after school, you earned $12.00 for four hours of baby-sitting. Last week, you baby-sat four hours. How much extra money can you earn if you cut the grass and baby-sit two hours next week?

What is the real question here? Let's work through the steps together.
Step 1: Cross out unimportant words and circle key words.

2. ~~You receive an allowance of $5.00 per week. If you do the laundry, you earn an extra $5.00 per week.~~ If you cut the grass, you get an extra $3.00 per week. When you took care of your younger brother after school, you earned $12.00 for four hours of baby-sitting. ~~Last week you baby-sat four hours.~~ How much extra money can you earn if you cut the grass and baby-sit two hours next week?

The only important facts are CUT GRASS = $3.00, BABY-SIT = $3.00 per hour ($12/4 hr = $3 per hour), TOTAL BABY-SITTING TIME = 2 HOURS.

Step 2: The real question

The real question is "how much extra money to cut the grass and baby-sit two hours?"

The real question can be restated like this: "What is $3.00 (the baby-sitting hourly rate of pay) x 2 (hours baby-sitting) + $3.00 (the wage for cutting grass)?"

When you answer the real question correctly, you will get the correct answer of $9.00.

There are two important things to remember. First, it is likely that many of the questions will have more words in them than those that are relevant to the real question. You will need to cross out these words so they don't distract you. Second, there are no trick questions on the test. Sure, there are some hard questions, but if you use the show what you know® techniques, answer the real question, and have at least some knowledge about the answer, you should do just fine.

Don't Waste Your Energy!
You get plenty of time to take this assessment. Don't rush yourself and spend all your energy trying to race the other students. Also, don't get stuck in a rut on one question by going over it again and again. Just rule out the wrong answers, select the best answer, and go on. Otherwise, you'll waste important strength.

You may make simple mistakes, like marking the wrong answer in your test booklet. You're human like everyone else, you too could make a mistake. Always double check to make sure the answer you are marking is the one you are intending to mark. **Be that careful. There is no sense in missing any question because you weren't careful.**

A Final Tip on Questions and Answers

If you're really dedicated, you can learn to understand test questions and answers more fully by making up some questions and answers yourself. Use the information on the topics we cover in the different sections of this book. Create some of your own questions, making sure to add "extra" words to some of the stories in the questions. Then make up answers that are there because they are the answers you would get if you made easy to make mistakes. For example, if you make up a question for reading, and the topic is knowing what a word means from its context, then make some of the answers other meanings for the word, but ones that are not consistent with the context. Each time you write the answers, write down why the wrong answers are wrong and why the right answer is correct. Then later, in a couple of days, answer several of these questions. Read all the answers, and if you get the wrong answer, be sure to understand the common, or easy-to-make, mistake you made. This method is a great tool; it helps you understand how to work with the questions, and it will reduce your fear of taking the WASL. By using this tool, you will gain confidence, knowledge, and test-taking skills, and be successful on the WASL!

Listening

Introduction

The Listening section of the Washington Assessment of Student Learning (WASL) measures how well you understand what you hear. It is important to practice your listening skills so you can become a better listener. Even though the passages and the questions are similar, listening skills are much different than reading skills. When you listen, you need to remember details about what you are hearing. When you read, you can see the words in front of you, and you can refer back to the passage to help you answer the questions.

For this section of the WASL, you will answer questions about a passage that is read to you. Most of these questions will be multiple-choice questions that will ask you to pick the best answer from four choices. At most, there will be two short-answer questions that will require you to write your responses in sentences or in a paragraph. These questions are not meant to trick you in any way. They are written clearly so you have the best chance to answer them correctly.

When you come to this section of the book, make sure not to look at the reading passages. For the Listening assessment, your teacher or parent will read the passages to you aloud, and you will answer questions on each passage. The questions in this chapter start on the page after the passage so you can answer the questions without having to worry about accidentally seeing the passage. If you need to, you can cover the passage with a sheet of paper. While you are listening, pay close attention to the details in the passage to help you answer the questions. You can take notes during and after the reading. Jot down key words that will help spark your memory. You can use any form of note taking you prefer.

You will complete 23 practice items designed to help you practice your test-taking skills. Following these practice items, there is one sample assessment test, Day One, which has been created to simulate the experience of taking the WASL Listening test. An additional practice test is also available.

Practice Items

Listening Activity 1

Directions: DO NOT READ THIS PASSAGE. Have your teacher or a parent read it to you. Listen as "Skateboarders' Dilemma" is read aloud to you. After the reading, you will answer questions based on what you have heard. You may take notes during and after the reading.

Skateboarders' Dilemma

Skateboarders in our community are treated unfairly. Skateboarding is a wholesome sport. My peers are worried that skateboarding is being banned throughout our town.

We have searched everywhere for a place to skateboard and are constantly told we cannot skate on private or public property. Last summer, we skateboarded on the empty school parking lot. We were always respectful. This summer, signs were posted stating skateboarding was banned on school grounds. Other parking lots, public places, and public parks also had signs indicating skateboarding was prohibited. If you are going to ban skateboarding from public places, please give kids somewhere they can skateboard.

Two years ago, the community of Sierra raised money to build a skateboarding complex. Teens, their families, members of the Parks and Recreation Board, the mayor, and his staff all pitched in. Skateboarders respect the area and invite community members to watch them practice. The area helps everyone appreciate this unique sport.

Our community should consider building a skateboarding area that would provide a safe place for kids to skateboard and have fun. Using Sierra as an example, we can see that a skateboarding area is a good idea for our town.

1. Which phrase best defines how the author feels about skateboarding?

    ○ A. Skateboarding is a wholesome sport.
    ○ B. Skateboarding is a damaging sport.
    ○ C. Skateboarding should be banned.
    ○ D. Skateboarders are disrespectful.

2. What do the author and his friends consider unfair treatment of skateboarders?

    ○ A. allowing skateboarders to skate in empty parking lots
    ○ B. banning skateboarding from public places without providing an alternative for skateboarders
    ○ C. providing skateboarders a place to skateboard
    ○ D. banning joggers from the public parks

3. Which one of the following phrases may be true of the people responsible for placing the ban on skateboarding?

    ○ A. they feel skateboarders damage property
    ○ B. they consider skateboarding a wholesome sport
    ○ C. they realize a skateboarding area is needed in their community
    ○ D. they want all skateboarders to start riding bikes

4. Considering the title "Skateboarders' Dilemma," which one of the following sentences is the main idea?

    ○ A. "Skateboarding is a wholesome sport."
    ○ B. "Two years ago, the community of Sierra raised money to build a skateboarding complex."
    ○ C. "My peers are worried that skateboarding is being banned throughout our town."
    ○ D. "We were always respectful."

5. Which one of the following statements would the author most likely support?

    ○ A. Skateboarding should be banned from public parks.
    ○ B. Other sports should be banned from public parks.
    ○ C. The community should provide an area for skateboarders.
    ○ D. It will cost too much money to build a skateboarding area.

6. Which solution would the author find most acceptable?

   ○ A. Ban all sports from public property.
   ○ B. Allow teens to skateboard in public parking lots.
   ○ C. Close sections of the parks for skateboarding only.
   ○ D. Encourage the community to work together to raise money to build a skateboarding
        area for teens.

7. Explain what the community of Sierra did for their teens.

   _____

   _____

   _____

   _____

8. What solution does the author offer that would solve the skateboarders' dilemma?

   _____

   _____

   _____

   _____

Listening Activity 2

Directions: DO NOT READ THIS PASSAGE. Have your teacher or a parent read it to you. Listen as "The Big Change" is read aloud to you. After the reading, you will answer questions based on what you have heard. You may take notes during and after the reading.

The Big Change

"Good luck," Mom said cheerfully as I got out of our van. I turned around toward a long row of steps leading to two enormous wooden doors. Unfamiliar students rushed by me, laughing and talking. I urged my legs up the numerous steps and reached for the left door. It flung open before I touched it. Faces hurried past me. "New girl," someone said as I walked through the right door and down the long hallway. A short, blonde girl smiled at me. I walked toward her.

"I'm Ashley," she said warmly. "Are you Karen? I volunteered to show you around. I was a new student last year. I hope I can make your first day easier."

"Thanks, I have no idea where to go." My heart rate slowed. I felt better. Ashley showed me around and introduced me to my new teachers and classmates. They were very friendly. Ashley told me about an important school tradition, "Always use the right door. You'll always be 'right' if you use the right door." We both laughed when I told her I learned that lesson the hard way. Maybe this new school won't be so bad after all.

9. Which word best describes how the author feels when she gets out of her mom's van?

   ○ A. cheerful
   ○ B. nervous
   ○ C. angry
   ○ D. sad

10. What is Karen's reaction after talking with Ashley?

   ○ A. Her heart rate slows and she feels better.
   ○ B. Her stomach feels queasy like she is going to get sick.
   ○ C. She is afraid to approach her and wants to turn around.
   ○ D. She is upset that Ashley didn't meet her at the steps.

11. What important school tradition did Ashley share with Karen?

   ○ A. Always arrive on time.
   ○ B. Never run in the halls.
   ○ C. Always use the "right" door.
   ○ D. Wear school colors on Fridays.

12. Which sentence best paraphrases Karen's first day at her new school?

   ○ A. Even though Karen was confused and unsure at first, Ashley was able to help her feel at ease after spending the day with her.
   ○ B. Karen never did figure out where to go and decided she would never be able to learn the school's traditions.
   ○ C. Karen wanted to return to her other school because she didn't like the teachers or students.
   ○ D. After almost getting run over by all the students in the hall, Karen decided she would need to arrive earlier to find her way around the new school.

13. How do you think Karen will feel when she comes to school on the second day?

   ○ A. angry
   ○ B. frightened
   ○ C. confident
   ○ D. unsure

14. Ashley told Karen about an important school tradition. Why did Karen tell Ashley she learned that lesson the hard way? Use an example from the selection to support your answer.

_____

_____

_____

_____

_____

_____

15. Explain why the author closed her personal narrative with the following sentence, "Maybe this new school won't be so bad after all."

_____

_____

_____

_____

_____

_____

Listening Activity 3

Directions: DO NOT READ THIS PASSAGE. Have your teacher or a parent read it to you. Listen as the following Letter to the Editor is read aloud to you. After the reading, you will answer questions based on what you have heard. You may take notes during and after the reading.

September 5, 2000

Dear Editor,

I am writing this letter to bring to your attention the need for more sidewalks in our city's neighborhoods. Because of the lack of sidewalks, our residents risk danger each time they walk, jog, or inline skate on city streets.

Traffic is becoming more congested as drivers come to near halts when attempting to pass a runner or cyclist. I am concerned for people's safety, especially when pedestrians and motorists are forced to use the same roadways.

Neighborhoods throughout our community consist of families, many with young children. It is important for these children to have safe areas in which to skate and walk. Many children, not permitted on streets, walk through neighbors' lawns.

There are several people in my neighborhood whose grass is being trampled because of repeated foot traffic from neighborhood kids. These community members would really appreciate more sidewalks for children to use.

We must make a change for the safety and convenience of our community members. My grandfather told me a Development Trust was set up to be used to enrich this community. Please consider using money from the trust to build more sidewalks. Thank you for considering my recommendation.

Sincerely,

Nadia Rees

16. Which one of the following would be an opinion of the author?

    ○ A. There are enough sidewalks in our community.
    ○ B. The lack of sidewalks makes it inconvenient for drivers, cyclists, and runners.
    ○ C. Drivers should be forced to stop when a runner or cyclist is on the road.
    ○ D. There are no safety issues concerning the lack of sidewalks in our community.

17. Which one of the following would the author consider unsafe?

    ○ A. children walking through neighbors' yards
    ○ B. residents getting exercise
    ○ C. drivers attempting to pass a runner or cyclist
    ○ D. residents walking on sidewalks

18. Who is the intended audience for this letter?

    ○ A. children
    ○ B. the author's grandfather
    ○ C. athletes
    ○ D. the editor of the local newspaper, community leaders, and community members

19. Who told the author about the Development Trust?

    ○ A. the author's neighbor
    ○ B. the neighborhood children
    ○ C. the author's grandfather
    ○ D. the author's brother

20. How does the author feel about children walking on neighbors' lawns?

    ○ A. it ruins lawns
    ○ B. it provides a nice shortcut
    ○ C. it is trespassing
    ○ D. she has no feelings about it

21. After listening to the letter, what seems to be the reason for the lack of sidewalks?

   ○ A. It is easier to exercise in the street.
   ○ B. Drivers don't mind passing pedestrians using the street.
   ○ C. The community hasn't had enough money to build sidewalks.
   ○ D. People didn't want to pay for sidewalks in their neighborhoods.

22. If sidewalks are not built, name three consequences residents of this community will encounter.

   _____

   _____

   _____

   _____

   _____

   _____

23. In her letter, the author mentions a Development Trust. Explain what this trust money can be used for.

   _____

   _____

   _____

   _____

   _____

   _____

Listening Assessment: Day One and Additional Practice*

Directions: The Grade 7 Washington Assessment of Student Learning for Listening will take one day. This assessment will measure how well you understand what you hear.

Your teacher will read a passage aloud to you. You may take notes during and after the reading. You will not be able to look at the passage. When the teacher is finished reading the passage, you will be asked to answer questions about it. You will answer two types of questions. The first type of question will ask you to pick the correct answer from four choices. The second type of question will ask you to write your response in sentences or in a paragraph.

Remember to listen carefully and take good notes. You can use any form of note taking with which you feel comfortable. If you don't know the answer to a question, skip it and go back to it later. If you are finished early, check your work to make sure you have correctly answered the questions.

*Note: Beginning in 2003, the Listening Test may be extended to two days. To reflect this change, a second listening assessment has been provided as additional practice.

Day One

Directions: DO NOT READ THIS PASSAGE. Have your teacher or a parent read it to you. Listen as "Cesar Estrada Chavez" is read aloud to you. After the reading, you will answer questions based on what you have heard. You may take notes during and after the reading.

Cesar Estrada Chavez

Mexican descendent, Cesar Estrada Chavez, was born March 31, 1927, near Yuma, Arizona. In the 1930s, the Chavez family moved to California, becoming part of a migrant community traveling from farm to farm, harvesting crops. Farm workers had poor living conditions — long days and small pay. The Chavez family often slept in their car.

After eighth grade, Cesar quit school to work full-time in vineyards. He joined the Navy in 1944, fighting for two years in World War II. In 1946, he returned to California to work in the fields. Seeing a need for change, he joined an unsuccessful strike protesting low wages and poor working conditions. By 1952, Cesar was speaking throughout California, supporting farm workers' rights and urging Mexican-Americans to vote.

Cesar led a five-year strike of California grape-pickers in 1965, demanding higher wages and encouraging Americans to boycott grapes. The strike increased national awareness as Chavez rallied millions to support the farm workers' cause.

Cesar continued to fight for farm workers' rights and also fought against toxic pesticides used on produce. He advocated nonviolent protesting and became well respected throughout America. Even after his death, his legacy of establishing farm workers' rights continues today.

Go On ▶

1. What is the definition of the word *migrant*?

    ○ A. a farm worker who travels from farm to farm
    ○ B. someone who goes on strike
    ○ C. people who sleep in cars
    ○ D. someone who makes speeches

2. Which one of the following is an accurate description of Cesar Chavez?

    ○ A. He was a violent man.
    ○ B. He was a college graduate.
    ○ C. He was a nonviolent protester.
    ○ D. He was an only child.

3. Cesar Chavez led a successful strike in 1965. How long did that strike last?

    ○ A. 1 year
    ○ B. 5 years
    ○ C. 4 years
    ○ D. 3 years

4. Why did Cesar Chavez encourage Americans to boycott grapes?

    ○ A. to bring attention to the terrible conditions migrant workers faced
    ○ B. because the grapes tasted terrible
    ○ C. he didn't believe in making wine from grapes
    ○ D. to start a fight with the grape growers

5. What does the following statement from the passage imply?

    Even after his death, his legacy of establishing farm workers' rights continues today.

    ○ A. Farmers still do not have adequate conditions under which to work.
    ○ B. People continue to support nonviolent methods of protest in the fight for farm
       workers' rights.
    ○ C. Farm workers are treated fairly and are content with their conditions.
    ○ D. The work Cesar Chavez did for farm workers was quickly forgotten.

Go On ▶

6. Why did Cesar quit going to school after the 8th grade?

   ○ A. He didn't like school.
   ○ B. He wanted to join the Navy.
   ○ C. His family needed him to work in the fields.
   ○ D. He felt he had enough education.

7. Write a paragraph summarizing the main points of this selection in your own words. Be sure to include at least three points that you can remember from the passage in your summary.

   _____

   _____

   _____

   _____

   _____

   _____

   _____

   _____

8. After serving in the Navy, Cesar returned to working in the fields. What types of things do you think caused Cesar to see a need for change for farm workers?

   _____

   _____

   _____

   _____

   _____

STOP

Additional Practice

Directions: DO NOT READ THIS PASSAGE. Have your teacher or a parent read it to you. Listen as the Letter to the Editor is read aloud to you. After the reading, you will answer questions based on what you have heard. You may take notes during and after the reading.

May 30, 2001

Dear Editor:

I am writing to bring to your attention the need for a citywide effort to "clean up" our community. Litter is filling our streets, our parks, and our neighborhoods. Does anyone in City Hall have a plan for tackling this litter problem?

We need to set a positive image for members of our community. We need to let people know we are proud of where we live and littering in our community is wrong. I want my little brothers and sisters to grow up in a clean and safe community.

I am making three recommendations for officials in City Hall to consider regarding this littering problem:

1. Place more trashcans around the city to discourage people from disposing of their trash on the ground.
2. Pass a city law that fines anyone who litters.
3. Display "Don't Litter" and "Keep Our Neighborhood Clean" awareness signs throughout the city.

I hope that the officials in City Hall and the residents of our community will think long and hard about a solution to this growing litter problem.

Sincerely,

Everett Meyers

Go On ▶

1. With which statement would the author most likely agree?

   ○ A. Littering is a personal issue and not an issue for the community.
   ○ B. There shouldn't be a penalty for littering.
   ○ C. We don't need more trash cans.
   ○ D. City Hall needs a plan for tackling the litter problem.

2. The author mentions the need for a citywide effort to "clean up" the community. What would be considered citywide?

   ○ A. Only the residents that live near parks.
   ○ B. All residents in the community.
   ○ C. People at City Hall.
   ○ D. All the children that play in the community.

3. What could happen if this community continues to ignore the litter problem?

   ○ A. The community members will be proud of where they live.
   ○ B. The litter will disappear on its own.
   ○ C. People will want to live and work in this community.
   ○ D. People will think that littering is not wrong.

4. When the author asks if anyone in City Hall has a plan for tackling this litter problem, what does he mean?

   ○ A. He wants names of people from City Hall who are going to pick up litter.
   ○ B. He expects City Hall to solve the litter problem.
   ○ C. He wants to know if there has ever been a plan for litter control.
   ○ D. He is going to ask that these people be fired.

5. Who is the intended audience for this letter?

   ○ A. the mayor
   ○ B. employees of City Hall
   ○ C. people who litter
   ○ D. all members of the community

Go On ▶

6. What does it mean when the author asks the officials in City Hall and the residents of the community to "think long and hard" about a solution to the littering problem?

   ○ A. He is asking these people to think briefly about the littering problem.
   ○ B. He is asking these people to take the littering problem seriously and to work together for a solution.
   ○ C. He is asking these people just to think about the littering problem but not make any decisions.
   ○ D. He is asking these people to think about the littering problem and to be hard on those who litter.

7. What is one recommendation being made to City Hall? What might the author hope to accomplish by making this recommendation?

   _____

   _____

   _____

   _____

8. Explain two of the reasons the author states for why the community should get involved with litter control.

   _____

   _____

   _____

   _____

   _____

   _____

STOP

Reading

Introduction

The Reading section of the Washington Assessment of Student Learning (WASL) is designed to measure what you have learned in reading through the seventh grade. You will read fiction, nonfiction, poems, maps, advertisements, and other materials to show what you know about important reading concepts. Some of these concepts are understanding aspects of texts like theme, plot, and setting, interpreting vocabulary in texts, and identifying important ideas and supporting details.

The Reading section of this assessment will take two days. Each day, the test will take approximately 1 hour and 15 minutes broken into two parts. You will have a 15 minute break in between these two parts. It is OK if you need more time. There is no time limit, just an approximate amount of time.

After you read each passage, you will answer questions about it. Some questions will be multiple-choice and will ask you to pick the best answer out of four choices. Other questions will be short-answer items and will ask you to write responses in a couple sentences or in a paragraph. You will also be asked extended-response questions in which you write your answer in a couple paragraphs. You cannot use outside reference material to help you answer questions. The questions are written clearly so you can understand them. They are not meant to trick you in any way.

You will complete 30 practice items designed to help you practice your test-taking skills. Following these practice items, there are two sample assessment tests, Day One and Day Two, which have been created to simulate the experience of taking the WASL Reading test.

Practice Items

Directions: Read the following passage to answer questions 1 through 7.

A Family Thing
by Thomas J. Murphy

"Ryan, that's so cool!" I shouted. "Sure, they'll let me. My parents wouldn't keep me from the best adventure in the whole world. I'll talk to my mom right now. Then I'll call you later." I hung up the phone and spun around like a whirling top.

"Bee in your britches, Cody?" Stacey asked.

Stacey is my sister and second-best friend, after Ryan. "Guess what Stacey? Ryan asked me to go with him and his dad on a whitewater canoeing trip. Awesome, huh?"

"In the middle of school?" she asked.

"That's the best part," I replied. "It's during spring break. Too bad, I won't miss any school, though," I added with a big grin. "I'll take pictures and tell you all about it when I get back. I can't believe this is happening to me."

"I'm happy for you," Stacey mumbled as she left the room.

What's with her? I wondered. But my mind refused to dwell on anything but the canoe trip. Shifting into high gear, I raced to find my mom. And boy did I. The sudden collision with her and the laundry basket failed to dampen my spirits. "Sorry," I gushed, stooping to help pick up the once-neatly-folded whites.

"I expect there is a reason for all this boisterousness," Mom said with a scowl.

My mouth overran my brain as I revealed my great news. "Isn't that the most awesome thing you've ever heard?" I declared.

"No doubt," Mom replied. "You'll need money, I suppose."

Taking that as a yes, I jumped into the air. "I have money — nineteen dollars and fifty cents."

"That's a start, I guess. Dad and I will provide the rest," she said. "When are you leaving?"

"Friday, after school lets out for break. Sorry I won't get to spend time with the family. Naturally, that is important to me," I added. I knew how she and Dad felt about our family spending time together during holidays and vacations. But this was different. This was whitewater canoeing!

"Looks like you've thought of everything," said my mom.

"Sure have," I replied, ignoring her *guess what you forgot voice*. "Thanks Mom. I have to call Ryan."

"Cody! The clothes," shouted my mom.

Eight steps from the laundry room, I noticed the basket still in my arms. "Oh, yeah." I ran back and plopped the clothesbasket in her outstretched hands, then fled for the phone.

Snatching it from the cradle, I punched the first button of Ryan's number. "Excuse me," came a voice over the phone.

"Oops. Sorry, Stacey. Didn't know you were on the other line. Can you please hurry? I have to call Ryan and tell him Mom said yes. I can go on the canoe trip."

A moment of silence greeted me. "Stacey? Did you hear me?"

"I heard you," she whispered. "I'll call you later, Tiffany." There was a sudden click in my ear, then another. "You don't have to hang up right now, just pretty soon," I said. But the line was dead. Stacey was already gone.

Shrugging, I whizzed through the numbers. Suddenly, while the phone was ringing, something hit me like a baseball bat. It was like when I eat ice cream too fast and it freezes my brain — that kind of something. "Oh, no!"

Slowly, I lowered the phone to its cradle. I realized why Stacey wasn't elated about my good news. Saturday — the day we would be on the river — was her birthday.

I walked to her bedroom. The door was closed. She would be on her bed, sobbing into her pillow. I knew then why Mom had used that tone of voice with me earlier. She hadn't wanted to question me or tell me I couldn't go. She'd wanted me to make that decision.

"Stacey, may I come in?" I pleaded, rapping gently on her door. No answer. I opened the door just a crack. "Stacey? Hey, I'm really sorry. I just forgot for a minute, that's all. No way will I go on that canoe trip this weekend."

Stacey finally rolled over and stared up at me. "You . . . you really did just forget? You didn't choose that trip over my birthday?"

"Of course not, Stacey. You know better than that!" Sure, I'd rather be in that canoe, I thought to myself. But Stacey had been excited for months about becoming a teenager. We had a big surprise party planned for her and everything. "There will be other canoe trips. But my sister will have only one thirteenth birthday."

Before I could stop her, Stacey lunged and gripped me in a bear hug, soaking me with alligator tears. "Hey, back off," I said, pretending to push her away.

Instead, she hugged me tighter. And I, trying to fight off the lump in my throat, hugged her right back.

1. What message is the author of this story trying to convey to readers?

   O A. There may be times you need to think about the feelings of others instead of your own feelings.
   O B. Going on a trip with a friend requires a great deal of responsibility.
   O C. It is important to ask for your parents' permission before going on a trip.
   O D. When you have a difficult decision to make, always put yourself first.

2. What are three ways the author gives clues to help develop the theme of the story? Explain your choices.

   _____

   _____

   _____

   _____

3. Using your own words, summarize what happens in this story.

   _____

   _____

   _____

4. Which one of the following ideas could you infer after reading "A Family Thing"?

   O A. Cody would rather be canoeing than spending time with his family.
   O B. Cody and Stacey have a good relationship.
   O C. Cody would do anything for his friends.
   O D. Cody has a difficult time making decisions.

5. What do you think Cody will tell Ryan about the canoe trip? Explain your answer.

   _____

   _____

   _____

6. What does Stacey mean when she asks Cody, "Bee in your britches?"

    ○ A. She is using the phrase to teach Cody that the letter "B" is the first letter used in the word "britches."
    ○ B. She wants to know if there is an insect in Cody's pants causing him to jump.
    ○ C. She is asking if he has a bad feeling about something because he is acting upset.
    ○ D. She is using a figure of speech to refer to Cody's quick and excited movements.

7. Why does the author use the word *boisterousness* when describing Cody's behavior in paragraph eight?

    ○ A. The author uses this word to show that Cody is calm and quiet.
    ○ B. The author uses this word to show that Cody is rough and lively.
    ○ C. The author uses this word to show that Cody is gentle and silent.
    ○ D. The author uses this word to show that Cody is angry and loud.

Directions: Read the following passage to answer questions 8 through 13.

New Frontier
by Corinne Pratz

I'm going to die before we get there, Jack thought to himself as his left leg fell asleep for the fifth time since the last stop. He tried to shift around only to hear loud protests from his younger sister who was sitting beside him dozing off from the lull of the tires rolling on pavement. Geez! Why do I have to have such long legs? Yup, I'm going to die, or go insane — one of the two for sure.

Jack positioned his leg and instantly an entourage of pins and needles began sweeping over as it began to 'wake up.' He hadn't been too sure about this move to begin with. Now he was even more pessimistic. Even though it was only the second day, it felt like he had been crammed into his family's small car with his sister and two cats for a year. That was another thing, the cats. Jack liked them fine enough, but being stuck with them in small quarters was not exactly his idea of fun. Every single time they stopped, Mom loudly instructed, "Watch the cats! Watch the cats! Watch the cats!" Ah, yeah Mom. We all know that by now, after fifty stops, Jack thought.

He strained his neck toward the road ahead and spotted the moving van. It rolled along jam-packed with everything his family owned. It was Jack's brother's turn to ride with Dad in the van. The sweet, roomy, air-conditioned van. Next, it was his sister's turn and then his again. He shifted again. Probably more comfortable in the back of the van with all the furniture! Jack grumbled to himself, "My legs are going to snap off from lack of blood flow by the time it's my turn again!"

Jack thought about his buddies left long behind. He missed them already. He wondered what the kids would be like at the new place. He had no idea. In fact, he couldn't even imagine the new place. His parents had shown him pictures, but that hardly satisfied his curiosity. At times, he was filled with such dread, it was hard to breathe. Yet at other times, he felt kind of excited at the thought of a totally new and different place to explore.

"Hey, kids! Look at the ocean! We're almost at the ferries," Mom announced.

Jack popped his head up and looked out of the window. Never before had he seen such a sight! Miles and miles of clear blue water stretched out before them, rippling with waves and dotted with ships of all sizes.

Holy smokes! This was incredible! He was so taken that he didn't contribute to the chatter that was now filling the car. His eyes darted from boats to the great horizon. Try as he might, Jack could not take everything in as quickly as he wanted.

"Wow! Isn't it something? So beautiful! And the best part is, we only have to take the ferry and we'll be there!"

That got his attention. We're almost there? Yes!

8. Which one of the following provides the setting for the story?

    ○ A. the front seat of a moving van
    ○ B. a bedroom in a new house
    ○ C. the back seat of a family car
    ○ D. a crowded bench on a ferry

9. Choose two words that describe the main character. Tell what the main character says or does that made you choose these words. Support your answer with evidence from the text.

    _____

    _____

    _____

    _____

10. If this story were told from the mother's point of view, how might it be different?

_____

_____

_____

_____

_____

11. Which of the following sentences from the story best explains why Jack thinks to himself, "Holy Smokes! This is incredible!"

   ○ A. "He strained his neck toward the road ahead and spotted the moving van."
   ○ B. "His parents had shown him pictures of the new place."
   ○ C. "Mom announced, 'Hey, kids! Look at the ocean! We're almost at the ferries!'"
   ○ D. "Mom loudly instructed, 'Watch the cats! Watch the cats! Watch the cats!'"

12. Tell why Jack would rather be riding in the van with his father than in the family car. Use details from the story to support your answer.

_____

_____

_____

_____

13. In the fourth paragraph, the narrator mentions that Jack sometimes has a feeling of dread. What are three thoughts Jack has had that caused his feelings?

_____

_____

_____

_____

Directions: Read the following two passages, "Amelia Earhart" and "Paper Boy," to answer questions 14 and 15.

Amelia Earhart
by Liz Donegan

The mysterious disappearance of Amelia Earhart left millions in shock. Earhart was a renowned aviator who broke several records. Earhart was an extraordinary woman who experienced great fame and popularity in her lifetime. She was famous around the world. She even socialized with President Roosevelt and his wife Eleanor. Her mysterious disappearance is even more amazing than her fabulously exciting life.

Earhart's childhood was different from most children's in the early 20th century. Her family moved frequently, enabling Earhart to see much more of the country than most other children. She saw her first

airplane when she was just ten-years-old. Several years later, she came in close contact with another airplane at a stunt-flying exhibition. This plane made a lasting impression on young Earhart. She was determined to learn to fly when she was older. When Earhart finished high school, she became a nurse in Canada during World War I. After the war, Earhart returned to the United States to attend Columbia University. All this time, her desire to fly grew. By 1921, at the age of 25, Earhart earned her pilot's license. She was one of a handful of women in the world to earn this achievement.

In 1922, Earhart bought her first plane, *Kinnear Canary,* and broke her first flying record shortly afterward for flying at the highest altitude. She flew her plane straight up, until the plane reached 14,000 feet and the engine failed. Even with all of Earhart's skill and fame, pilot jobs were difficult to come by, especially for women. Eventually, Earhart sold her plane to buy a car in which she and her mother traveled cross-country from California to Boston. Her second aviation record was soon to be set, however, when Captain H. H. Railey and publisher George Putnam asked her to make a trip across the Atlantic Ocean. On June 17, 1928, Earhart, and two co-pilots, William Stultz and Louis Gordon, set out to cross the Atlantic. It took them two days starting in Trepassey, Newfoundland, and ending in Burry Port, Wales. Earhart was the first woman to ever cross the Atlantic by air. She was instantaneously famous.

Because of Earhart's tremendous fame, George Putnam, who she would later marry, asked her to write a book about her experience crossing the Atlantic. The book, *Twenty Hours, 40 Minutes*, was so successful that Earhart quickly had the money to buy herself another airplane. Earhart was back to setting records the way she wanted to, as the pilot. She became the first woman to fly solo across the

United States, across the Pacific Ocean, and across the Atlantic Ocean. These records gained Earhart even greater fame. She used this fame to speak to young women, encouraging them to follow their dreams and work hard. In 1937, she made the announcement that she wanted to fly around the world at the equator.

Earhart's attempt to fly around the world at the equator was the first of its kind and the last trip she would ever take. The 29,000-mile trip began on June 1, 1937 and was scheduled to end in Oakland, California, on July 4, 1937. Amelia Earhart and her navigator, Fred Noonan, successfully completed 22,000 miles of the trip in 29 days. The final leg of the trip was to be from Lae, Papua New Guinea, to Oakland, California, 7,000 miles across the Pacific Ocean. Unfortunately, Earhart's plane, *Electra*, could not hold enough fuel for this trip, so they had to stop for fuel somewhere between the two points. Howland Island was determined to be the fuel stop for Earhart and Noonan. Howland Island, however was only one-mile long, and a half-mile wide. The day Earhart and Noonan were to stop for fuel on Howland Island was rainy, foggy, and windy. A U.S. Coast Guard ship called *Itasca* was to be in the waters around Howland Island to give Earhart important weather information. Tragically, something was wrong with *Itasca's* radio. The ship's radio operator could hear Earhart desperately asking for weather information, but he was unable to send her what she needed. Finally, *Itasca* received no more word from *Electra*. Earhart and Noonan had disappeared.

President Roosevelt called out the largest air and sea search in history: 4,000 troops, 9 ships, and 66 planes. Unfortunately, the late 1930s were a time of mistrust, as a world war was brewing. The United States and Japan were not on friendly terms, and the Japanese controlled much of the Pacific Ocean. The Japanese refused to allow American troops to search Japanese waters, saying they would search for Earhart themselves. After 16 days, the Navy called off the search. Earhart and Noonan were presumed dead. Two years later, World War II began overseas. News of Earhart and Noonan faded away.

Several people do not believe that Earhart died in a plane crash. In 1943, the movie *Flight for Freedom* was released. It told a story almost identical to Earhart's life. The movie stated that the female pilot was working for the Navy as a spy against the Japanese. Many people believed this, despite the Navy's denial of the story. Even Earhart's own mother believes her daughter was working for the government when she disappeared. Several more witnesses have come forward to tell the same story. After years of investigation, no conclusive evidence has been found to prove that Earhart was a spy captured by the Japanese. Another story surfaced that Earhart and Noonan did crash but were rescued and taken as prisoners of war. The story was investigated, a book was written, but again, no conclusive evidence was found to prove the story. In 1970, Joe Klaas wrote a book titled *Amelia Earhart Lives*. In it, he claimed that Earhart was living disguised as a New Jersey housewife. Irene Bolam, the supposed living Amelia Earhart, looked like Earhart and flew airplanes but did not claim to be Earhart. In fact, she sued the publisher of the book, and it was taken out of stores. Even after all these years and all these stories, many people still believe that something, other than a plane crash, happened to Earhart. Her body was never found. Wreckage from her plane was never found. The mystery of the disappearance of Amelia Earhart remains unsolved.

Paper Boy
by Lawrence Schimel

"There is no substitute for hard work,"
   Thomas Alva Edison liked to say
when people asked him how he found
   the energy to invent so many things.

He was always working, since he was
   very young, earning money to buy
chemicals and supplies for his experiments.
   When he was twelve-years-old

he had an idea: people on the train
   from Port Huron to Detroit
would be restless and hungry
   during the long, uneventful journey.

So he decided to sell newspapers
   and magazines and fruit and candy
to passengers on the train.
   He woke early each morning,

to buy that day's newspapers,
   as well as fresh fruit and candies,
and be on board the 7 a.m. train.
   When the train reached Detroit

at 10 a.m., he'd go to the library
   and read science books, thinking up
new experiments to try on Sundays,
   which was his only day off.

At 6:30 p.m., he was on the train again
   heading from Detroit back to Port Huron,
with a batch of new Detroit newspapers
   and more fruit and candy to sell along the way.

He didn't get home until 10 p.m.,
   and was exhausted after such a long day
of hard work. He ate dinner
   and went right to bed, since he had to be up

early the next morning, to catch the 7 a.m. train
   from Port Huron to Detroit.
Even when he was tired, he worked tirelessly,
   always wanting to do more.

He was earning lots of money for chemicals,
   but he had no time to work on experiments.
He noticed that the baggage car on the train
   was never full, so he asked for permission

to use the baggage car as a working space.
   He set up his chemicals
and beakers and tubes, a portable laboratory,
   and conducted experiments on the train

when he wasn't busy selling newspapers.
   For three years, he worked like this,
double-time, working on his own projects
   and working selling papers on the train.

And that's how he managed to invent so many
   wonderful and important things during his lifetime —
movie projectors and light bulbs, all sorts of things —
   he loved to work, and he worked constantly.

As I pedal my bicycle across town,
   delivering newspapers before school,
I think about Thomas Alva Edison
   who started as a paperboy when he was my age.

If I work hard, just like he did,
   who knows what things,
wonderful and important things,
   I might invent?

14. After reading the two passages, "Amelia Earhart" **and** "Paper Boy," how are Earhart's **and** Edison's feelings about their dreams similar?

   ○ A. Earhart's and Edison's feelings about needing fame and fortune were most important in achieving their goals.
   ○ B. Earhart and Edison felt that, without money, they would not be able to achieve their goals.
   ○ C. Both Earhart and Edison felt strongly about their goals and worked hard to achieve them.
   ○ D. Earhart and Edison both felt that they did not need to put much effort into achieving their goals.

15. Why was it important for Amelia Earhart **and** Thomas Edison to have money? Support your answer, for both Earhart and Edison, with evidence from the text.

_____

_____

_____

_____

Directions: Read the following information to answer questions 16 through 18.

Earhart's Around the World Flight Route

Earhart departed Oakland, California, on May 21, 1937, to meet her flying partner, Fred Noonan, in Miami, Florida. She disappeared between Lae, Papua New Guinea, and Howland Island on July 2, 1937. The map below shows the route Earhart and Noonan flew.

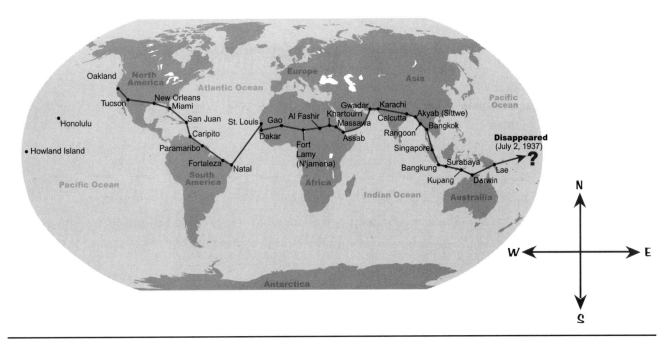

Schedule of Planned Stops on World Flight Route

Flight starts here:

Oakland, CA
Tucson, AZ
New Orleans, LA
Miami, FL
San Juan, Puerto Rico
Caripito, Venezuela
Paramaribo, Suriname
Fortaleza, Brazil
Natal, Brazil
St. Louis, Senegal ⎫
Dakar, Senegal   ⎬ then French
Gao, Mali   ⎪ West Africa
Fort Lamy, Niger ⎭
Al Fashir, Sudan
Khartoum, Sudan
Massawa, Ethiopia

Assab, Ethiopia
Gwadar, Pakistan (then part of India)
Karachi, Pakistan (then part of India)
Calcutta, India
Akyab, Myanmar (then Burma)
Rangoon, Myanmar (then Burma)
Bangkok, Thailand (then Siam)
Singapore, Malaysia
Bandung, Java, Indonesia
Soerabaja, Java, Indonesia
Kupang, Timor, Indonesia
Darwin, Australia
Lae, Papua New Guinea

failed to arrive at Howland Island, Honolulu, and Oakland, CA.

16. According to the map, if Amelia Earhart would have arrived at Howland Island, how many more scheduled stops would she have made before reaching Oakland?

○ A. 2 stops
○ B. 3 stops
○ C. 1 stop
○ D. 0 stops

17. Using the map, what was the last stop Earhart made before crossing to West Africa?

○ A. Fortaleza, Brazil
○ B. Paramaribo, Suriname
○ C. St. Louis, Senegal
○ D. Natal, Brazil

18. What important information does the "Schedule of Planned Stops on World Flight Route" provide?

_____

_____

Directions: Read the following passage to answer questions 19 through 25.

Charm and the Charmer
by Terry Miller Shannon

You should call me Charm. Everyone does. The only one who calls me by my real name, Henrietta, is my grandmother. Could be because that's her name, too. Maybe that name was okay when my grandmother was born, but how many young Henriettas do you know personally? My point exactly.

I never thought I'd get sick of the sound of my own nickname. But this summer, things changed around my house in a big way. I mean, a very big way. Suddenly, I was hearing 'Charm this,' and 'Charm that,' all the time. I took to riding my bike a lot, just to get away from it all.

To tell the truth, everyone else seemed quite happy. My mom was calmer and smiled a lot more. She's even took to baking, and trust me, that was a change. Her idea of making a fancy dinner used to be a can of chili beans mixed into cooked spaghetti noodles. You can imagine what she cooked when she was in a hurry. Next thing you know, that woman will be darning socks!

My new stepfather, Ralph, smiled even more than my mom. With the number of sparkling teeth I saw on a regular basis, you'd think I lived in a toothpaste commercial. But Ralph is OK. He's not my dad, but I don't think he's trying to be.

So, now we're getting to the real "charmer," if you'll excuse the pun. Did I ask to have a new stepfather? No. Did I ask to have a new stepbrother? Not on your life, no way, huh uh. I was perfectly happy with the way it had been for years. Just my mom and me.

Even when Mom told me she and Ralph were getting married, it didn't seem real. We'd spent lots of time with Ralph and Sam. We had fun together, mostly. But I couldn't picture what it would be like to have them around all the time.

Let me tell you about Sam. I haven't been around many four-year-old boys myself. Who would have expected him to adore a new, older sister? In fact, he liked me so much, it drove me crazy! From morning to night, Sam wanted to play with me, or have me read to him, or have me teach him to ride his new two-wheel bike, or watch television with me, etc. "Charm, Charm, Charm." That's when I started with the long bike rides. I mean, Sam is a cute kid, but in my previous life, with my mom, I was used to some quiet time. Now, the only way I could have some peace was to spend the day exploring on my bike.

As I'd pack my sandwich, fill a water bottle, and grab my helmet, I'd see a serious, round little face watching intently. "Charm," Sam would say. "Isn't it too bad I can't ride my two-wheel bike?"

"It sure is," I'd say distractedly. Then I'd leave.

August was passing. That meant my birthday was coming up. Since my birthday is August 30th, I usually get something I can wear to school. This year, I was hoping for a new backpack. I saw a great one in a catalog. I cleverly circled it and left the catalog on my mom's bedside table, open to that page.

About a week before my birthday, Sam started hinting, in his not-very-subtle four-year-old way, about the surprise he was going to give me. "Charm, you'll never guess what your birthday surprise is!" He'd say at breakfast. Or, at dinner he'd say, "Charm! I'll bet you can't wait for your birthday surprise!" Since I was spending so much of my time on the bike trails at the beach, I mostly saw him at breakfast and dinner. But he was always there to give me his sad wave as I'd take off on my bike. "Uh huh, right," I'd say. My mother would shoot me a warning look.

"He's working very hard on a surprise for you," she told me late one evening. Sam was in bed. "And, actually, I think you really are going to be surprised. He truly loves you, you know."

"Tell me about it." I sighed. After breakfast on the day of my birthday, my mom said, "Why don't we go ahead with your presents this morning? We'll have cake and ice cream tonight. That will stretch the fun out over the whole day. OK?"

"Yeah!" Sam yelled. He was really wound up. Ralph just smiled.

Mom had taken the backpack hint, I'm happy to say. It was just as good in person as it was in the catalog. When I opened a small, wrapped box from Ralph, I was thrilled to find a good halogen bike light. "Thanks, guys!" I said.

"We're not done yet," Ralph said, looking toward Sam. "Sam, how do you want to do this?"

"Charm has to stand on the front porch!" Sam's enthusiasm was ear-splitting. "Nobody but Charm."

"OK," I said, standing up.

"You have to wait a few minutes before you go out there!" Sam shouted, heading through the kitchen door into the garage. After a few minutes, Mom smiled at Ralph and lifted her eyebrows.

"It should be OK to go out now." Ralph said as he smiled at me. I stood on the front porch, waiting. The air was sweet tasting, with a slight salt tang from the nearby ocean. Minutes passed. Suddenly, out of the corner of my eye, I saw something coming toward me down the street. I turned to get a better look. The moving object was very slow and pretty wobbly. I just couldn't help smiling. But my smile didn't hold a candle to the one on Sam's face as he unsteadily rode his two-wheeler toward me.

"Surprise!" he shouted. "Happy birthday surprise! Now you'll never have to ride all alone!"

I was looking at a kid who had worked hard to give me a birthday surprise. But I somehow was also seeing a little brother who wouldn't stay little. I was picturing how he would change as he grew up. Maybe he wouldn't always adore me and "Charm" me. I was surprised to feel real sadness at that thought. Sure, it hadn't been my choice to have a brother, but now that I had one, I could either push him away or pull him close.

"Sam, this is the best surprise I've ever had, ever!" I said. "Let me get my bike. We'll take our first ride together!" And we did.

19. The author's tone in the first paragraph conveys which one of the following messages?

   ○ A. Charm likes her real name.
   ○ B. Charm wants to change her name.
   ○ C. Charm dislikes her grandmother.
   ○ D. Charm likes to be called 'Charm.'

20. Who is the audience for this story? How do you know? Support your answer with evidence from the story.

   _____

   _____

   _____

21. While reading the beginning of "Charm and the Charmer," you might make the generalization that Charm will never accept her new brother. Does the outcome of this story support this generalization? Why or why not? Support your answer with evidence from the story.

   _____

   _____

22. How does the author create anticipation for the birthday gift that Sam gives to Charm? What is Charm's reaction to the gift that Sam gives her? How does the author use this reaction to develop the theme of the story? Explain your answer using evidence from the story.

   _____

   _____

   _____

   _____

23. How will Charm most likely react to change in future situations?

   ○ A. She doesn't like change and never will.
   ○ B. She will want everything to be back to the way it was before her mom married Ralph.
   ○ C. She will be open to change because she realizes good things can come from it.
   ○ D. She will continue to avoid her younger brother.

24. Using details from the story, explain whether you would have reacted to Sam's present as Charm did.

_____

_____

25. How could you use what you learned about stepbrothers and stepsister in this story to give advice to a friend? Explain your answer with details from the passage.

_____

_____

_____

Directions: Read the following passage to answer questions 26 and 27.

Bala Sharks
by Anne Watkins

Bala sharks (*balantiocheilus melanopterus*) are not sharks at all, but they are called sharks because of their body shape and large dorsal fins. These freshwater fish are native to the waters of Thailand, Borneo, and Sumatra, where they are captured as tiny specimens to be sold for the pet trade. Also known as the tri-colored shark or silver shark, they are popular fish in the home aquarium.

The bala shark is easily recognized by its bright silver coloration, the big, whitish fins edged in black, its large scales, and its oversized, black eyes. Their graceful, streamlined bodies make bala sharks exciting to watch as they speed around their habitat.

These fish are sensitive to water quality and do best in a pH of 6.5 to 7 with water temperatures in the ranging from 72–82 degrees Fahrenheit. They have voracious appetites and accept most foods readily. Good quality flake foods, shrimp pellets, sinking goldfish pellets, vegetation, and the occasional feeding of live foods such as daphnia or blood worms will provide a well-rounded diet for the bala.

The covers on aquariums housing bala sharks must be snug fitting and secure. These fish are known to be strong jumpers and will leap out of a tank that is not tightly covered! Bala sharks, with their mild temperaments, make an excellent community fish when housed with tank mates of similar size and personality. They are non-aggressive and enjoy spending time darting from one end of the tank to the other in search of food.

Balas require large tanks to accommodate their active swimming habits. With proper care, well maintained tank water, a good diet, and a roomy aquarium, it is possible for the quick growing bala to reach sizes of up to 13 inches in length in a home aquarium. Because they grow so rapidly, it is wise to house them in as large an aquarium as possible. A 55-gallon tank would be a good choice for the bala.

You can find these fish in almost every pet store. Most balas for sale will be very small, but sometimes larger specimens are available. Bala sharks, with their flashy silver bodies and friendly personalities, make fascinating additions to any large, home aquarium.

26. Which one of the following is a major idea of the passage?

    ○ A. Bala sharks are sensitive to water quality.
    ○ B. Bala sharks require large tanks because they are active swimmers.
    ○ C. Bala sharks are popular fish in a home aquarium.
    ○ D. Bala sharks can reach sizes of up to 13 inches.

27. Identify an important idea in the passage. Explain why this idea is important.

_____

_____

_____

Directions: Read the following passage to answer questions 28 through 30.

Mystery of the Pyramids
by Timothy Kevin Perry

It has been said that all the knowledge of the Earth, its past, present, and future, is contained in the Pyramids. For centuries, scientists worldwide have marveled at their strangely excellent mathematical form and symmetry. Even Sir Isaac Newton came to investigate the Pyramids. His conclusions were astounding. Along with such scientific geniuses, many other professionals have also wondered about the uncanny mysteries these structures contain. Every time an analyst uncovers another amazing mystery about them, fresh new puzzles surface right behind it. The Egyptian Pyramids were built to serve as burial grounds for kings and queens. Traditional explanation also states that the Great Pyramid, in what is now Giza, served as the model for the others that followed. By the various dimensions and angles they possess, some feel these structures were used as celestial star markers. Other researchers go several steps further and suggest they were star markers built and designed by ancient extra-terrestrials.

These structures can be seen as far away as the moon. The *Apollo* astronauts even commented about this fact. One wonders, why would Egyptians design objects that can be viewed from outside the Earth's atmosphere? How would they have known about things like this during an era when most everyone believed the world was still flat and humans were the only beings in a flat-headed universe?

There are other uncanny aspects about these Pyramids as well. Built to face true North, the Great Pyramid is located at the precise center of Earth's land, and has an East–West axis which corresponds to the longest land parallel across the planet. The Great Pyramid is thirty times larger than New York's

Empire State Building. Many scientists today still can't understand how laborers working with primitive equipment could've actually placed these 15-ton stones with as much accuracy as modern machine methods. These strange, mysterious structures were built with an amazing 0.02 inch gap deliberately devised in between each stone. This arrangement allows enough space for the seal and glue to hold the stones together.

Throughout centuries, various world conquerors have been obsessed with the Pyramids and the mysterious secrets they contain. Napoleon was so fascinated with the Great Pyramid, that when his forces arrived there during the French Conquests, he deliberately spent a night inside it. It must've been a very scary night because Napoleon emerged, blanched white in shock. His experience was so devastating that he wouldn't discuss what had happened to him, with even his closest aides and officers.

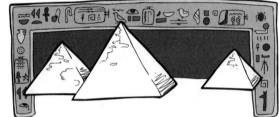

Whatever is the ultimate truth behind the Pyramids, one thing cannot be denied, they remain one of the most intriguing mysteries of the world.

28. Which sentence below tells why the following generalization is incorrect?

   Researchers will solve the mystery of the Pyramids.

   ○ A. The generalization is too broad to make, based on the information in the selection.
   ○ B. The generalization stated does not refer to information contained in the selection.
   ○ C. The generalization is faulty because it is based on opinion and not fact.
   ○ D. The generalization cannot be made because there is no mystery to solve.

29. Is the following generalization supported by the passage? Explain your answer with **two details** from the passage.

   Researchers will continue trying to solve the mystery of the Pyramids.

   _____

   _____

30. Name some techniques the author uses to make his point. Are these techniques effective? Why or why not?

   _____

   _____

   _____

Reading Assessment:
Day One and Day Two

Directions: The Grade 7 Washington Assessment of Student Learning for Reading will take two days. You will read stories and reading passages and then answer questions about them. Some questions will ask you to pick the best answer, and other questions will ask you to write your response. You will mark or write your answers directly in the test booklet.

Remember to take your time while reading each passage. You may refer to the passage as often as needed. Read each question carefully, and choose the answer you think is best. For questions asking for a written response, make sure to write your answers neatly. You may skip a question for which you do not know the answer and go back to it later. Do not turn the page when you see the word **STOP**. If you finish early, go back and check your work.

Day One

Directions: Read the following passage to answer questions 1 through 7.

The Rescue of the Nine-Banded Rabbit-Turtle
by Gail Blasser Riley

Many thousands of years ago, the Nine-Banded One surveyed the mountainous countryside as he skittered across the land on legs so short they appeared barely able to propel his strange body. The giant ground sloth and mastodons paid little attention to him as he traveled across the kingdom. While the dire wolves and the saber-tooth cats hissed at and fought against one another, the Nine-Banded One traveled by, unnoticed in the background.

The Nine-Banded One knew he should feel thankful and relieved, as he had no natural predators. Instead, relief had long ago given way to quiet anger. Sorrow and emptiness mixed to form a terrible ache in his heart. He was lonely. Though he had been told a long time before that others of his kind existed, he had yet to discover them, and he grew frustrated in his search.

One day, the Nine-Banded One's search led him toward the land of the human, a land said to hold great wonders but also torture and misery for all those who dared enter.

The Nine-Banded One traveled rough terrain for days. Finally, he arrived at the land of the human. As he crossed into this forbidden territory, the Nine-Banded One stopped in his tracks, raised his head, and flared his nostrils. The strange new scents filled him with fear and excitement all at once.

As he approached, the humans who saw the Nine-Banded One cried out shrill sounds that pierced the creature's tender ears. The humans raced away and cowered. They crouched behind rocks and trees as they viewed this strange armored being. For a short while, the humans watched and talked amongst themselves.

Soon, however, as the setting Sun's blaze illuminated the clearing, the humans crept slowly forward to investigate this new life form that had entered their kingdom. One by one, they reached out to brush a finger across the creature's back. Each time, the Nine-Banded One tingled warmly to the touch and inched forward, seeking more of this strange, delightful feeling.

Go On ▶

Though the humans at first pulled back in fear of this unknown skin, their curiosity gradually overtook their cowardice and they came to investigate again and again. "Rough," boomed one human. He touched the unusual hide, looked at his hand and looked back to the hide once more.

"Bumpy," another of these upright creatures declared.

These speech sounds pleased the Nine-Banded One. He began to feel comfortable and welcome. In time, the humans came often to stroke the creature and share their love and earthly belongings. They seemed to enjoy his playful antics and his generous return of affection. Seeking a name for their new companion, the humans explored many possibilities.

"He bears nine bands," observed one human.

"He resembles the rabbits and turtles of our land," offered another.

"We shall call him 'Nine-Banded Rabbit-Turtle,'" decreed a wise one.

But, as humans tend to do, another of their kind challenged the decree. "He is an armored one. We shall call him 'The Armored One.'"

Though the new creature would always be "The Nine-Banded Rabbit-Turtle" to many, "The Armored One" became his official name.

The Armored One lived for a joyful period in the presence of the humans, honored and held dear by all who came to know him.

This joy was short-lived, however. The Armored One soon fell prey to a human virus, a sickness it had never encountered in its own kingdom. The remedies offered by the humans proved worthless and the Armored One soon grew increasingly ill.

As the days passed, the Armored One could scarcely move about. The humans offered wise remarks, advising the Armored One to return to his homeland, believing that the creature might in some way shed this illness in his natural habitat.

But the Armored One had grown to cherish these humans who had made him the center of their world, who had stroked him, and loved him, and tended to him in a way that those who inhabited his native land never had.

In time, as he fought his sickness, the Armored One came to be known as the Armored Ill One. He lived out his last days in the land of those who had loved and cared for him.

Go On ▶

1. Why was the Nine-Banded One searching for his kind?

   ○ A. He didn't have natural predators.
   ○ B. The giant ground sloth didn't pay attention to him.
   ○ C. He was lonely.
   ○ D. He wanted to see the land of the human.

2. What does the author mean when she describes the land of the human as *forbidden territory*?

   ○ A. The terrain is rough.
   ○ B. The land holds torture and misery.
   ○ C. The land was far away.
   ○ D. The humans creep around.

3. Why did the Nine-Banded One die?

   ○ A. He was lonely.
   ○ B. He contracted a human virus.
   ○ C. He was killed by a natural predator.
   ○ D. He encountered a sickness from his homeland.

4. Which one of the following places provides the setting for the story?

   ○ A. Hundreds of years ago in the hot and dry desert.
   ○ B. Many thousand of years ago in the mountainous countryside.
   ○ C. An illuminated clearing.
   ○ D. A sandy beach along the ocean.

5. Explain why the Nine-Banded One traveled to the land of the humans. Use two details from the story to support your answer.

   _____

   _____

   _____

   _____

Go On ▶

6. What did the humans do that made the Nine-Banded One feel comfortable and welcome in their land? Use three details from the story to support your answer.

_____

_____

_____

_____

_____

7. Why did the Nine-Banded One ignore the remarks from the humans who were advising him to return to his homeland?

_____

_____

_____

_____

_____

Go On ▶

Directions: Read the following passage to answer questions 8 through 12.

The Potato Chip Man
by William I. Lengeman III

For as long as he could remember, Philip Rawletta loved potato chips. He loved 'em like a son . . . could have eaten 'em for a living. Even now, as he was approaching his fourth decade of life, Philip could think of nothing he loved more. Oh sure, there were his mother and sisters, his grandmother, and Emily, his soon-to-be wife. But there was no comparison there. It was like comparing apples and concrete.

It seemed absurd. It was only when he was eating chips that he was truly happy. Philip attacked a bag of potato chips with such a frenzy, that in no time he could reduce it to specks of dust in the bottom of the grease-coated bag. Then, of course, he drank down the crumbs, coughing and choking as he accidentally inhaled a few, and wincing with pleasure as the salt warmed his tongue.

Philip was not picky when to it came to potato chips. Anything would do: plain old garden-variety chips, ruffled Cajun spice, grainy sour cream and onion. He loved the nice, uniform ones that came packed in a cylinder as well as the thick gourmet-styled waffle chips that he could buy at the health store.

It simply did not matter. If it was a chip, it was fair game. Philip gobbled them all down, to borrow his mother's words, "like they were going out of style."

His sisters, who were less polite, called him "piggish" and "disgusting," while Philip munched away contentedly, ignoring them.

More than once, as she watched him tear into a bag, his grandmother remarked, "one of these days, you're gonna turn into a potato chip." Philip always laughed and kept cramming handfuls of potato chips into his face.

Philip's obsession snowballed as he grew older. Alone in his apartment, he occasionally ate nothing but chips for a meal, substituting different types for the various courses.

This was a rare treat at first. But soon Philip's self-restraint began to crumble. One chip feast a month gave way to two or three. Then it was once a week, and not long after that, twice. After six months in his new apartment, he was up to one meal a day of nothing but chips. He was downing as many as five large bags a day. The grocery store clerks often looked at his cart and asked, "Having a picnic?" Philip would smile and nod.

Philip worried about his health. But it seemed there was no turning back. He tried to take care of himself. He switched to fat-free chips at lunch and no-salt chips at dinner on Mondays, Wednesdays, Fridays, and every other Sunday. He upped his intake of vitamins, minerals and amino acids, and drank more water. He exercised more regularly.

Go On ▶

One cold, clear Saturday afternoon, in early November, Philip outdid himself. He devoured three giant bags of chips — BBQ, salt and vinegar, and ranch. He felt so bloated he was sure he would get sick. But he didn't. Instead he settled on the couch and slipped off into a deep sleep in front of a college football game.

As he was dreaming, he tried to swing a leg over the edge of the couch. But the other leg came with it . . . uninvited. Philip realized that his legs were fused together. He could see faint ridges running along his arm. Then he noticed that these creases were all over his body. They were neat and uniform, spaced about one inch apart, and ran from north to south on his legs, arms, stomach, chest, and, as far as he could tell, on his back. Philip's body was also thinner and wider. His arms and fingers had all but disappeared. After a half hour of struggle, he made his way to the bathroom, falling many times on the way. He was shocked when he looked into the mirror. He realized he was dreaming and prayed to wake up.

His body was getting stiffer as he stood there. Philip could barely bend over enough to look at his body. It was thin and rounded and curved forward at both the top and bottom. It was hard for him to keep his balance. He fell forward, striking what was left of his head on the sink. He woke up. He remembered what his grandmother had said. He'd have to give her a call and tell her all about his dream. They'd have a good laugh, and he would cut down on the potato chips.

8. What is the message the author wants readers of this story to know?

   ○ A. Don't fall asleep in front of the TV.
   ○ B. Don't eat in front of your grandmother.
   ○ C. Don't overdo a good thing.
   ○ D. Don't live alone in an apartment.

9. Which one of the following will Phillip most likely say to his grandmother when he wakes up?

   ○ A. He will tell her about the dream of becoming a potato chip.
   ○ B. He will tell her to bring over more potato chips.
   ○ C. He will tell her who won the football game.
   ○ D. He will tell her to mind her own business from now on.

10. The word "self-restraint" is found in the eighth paragraph. What does it mean?

   ○ A. the ability to eat a lot at one time and not get sick
   ○ B. the ability to hold yourself back from doing something you like to do
   ○ C. locking yourself in a room and never coming out
   ○ D. making people around you take away the things you like

11. What two words describe the main character, Philip? Use events from the story to explain why you chose these words.

   _____

   _____

   _____

12. What events led up to Philip having a dream about turning into a potato chip?

   _____

   _____

   _____

   _____

Directions: Read the following passage to answer questions 13 through 18.

Ellis Island: Passing Through Its Golden Gates Again
by Renie Szilak Burghardt

America has become the melting pot of the world. Your school or neighborhood probably has first generation immigrants that have come from countries like India, Vietnam, or even Russia. Your own family may have started out from one of those far away places many years ago.

These days, most immigrants no longer enter the United States through the Port of New York as they did for so many years in the past, like my family and I did on September 17, 1951, a day that is indelibly etched in my memory.

Go On ▶

Today, the enormous immigrant depot is a beautifully restored, popular tourist attraction: the Ellis Island Immigration Museum. Located in New York Harbor, two million tourists a year take the Ellis Island Ferry to visit this museum. One of the most famous landmarks in the world, over 100 million Americans — 40 percent of the population — can trace their ancestry in the United States to some man, woman, or child who passed from ship to Registry Room at Ellis Island, before beginning their new lives in their new country. My children are among those 100 million Americans.

My grandparents and I were Hungarian refugees when we boarded the Navy ship, *The General M. B. Stewart,* on September 7, 1951, along with hundreds of other refugees. After 10 harrowing days on a stormy Atlantic Ocean, we arrived in New York Harbor on September 17, 1951. I was fourteen-years-old and the only one in my family who spoke any English, thanks to the Refugee Camp School I had attended in Austria. Our first glimpse of Ellis Island and the New York skyline happened just before dawn broke. We were entranced by the trillions of lights sparkling out there, as if to welcome us.

As daylight broke, the refugees, now new immigrants with hope in their hearts, were tagged and ushered for processing to the main building of Ellis Island, an enormous hall filled with throngs of people. Greeted with many questions and finger pointing commands, I did my best to interpret some of it to my grandparents. However, my English was not all that good, since I had only studied it for two years.

The processing took many hours. Those that showed any signs of illness, went through rigorous medical exams. Many of them were turned back, for they only admitted able bodied, healthy people into this land known as America. Finally, after hours of questioning, probing, and waiting, we were released to a friendly looking man who would be our sponsor in this country. In his company, we would travel by train to Indiana to begin our new lives in America.

By the time my family and I arrived at Ellis Island, the immigration depot was in its last, waning years and would be closed down for good just three years later. Back in its hey day, in the early 1900s, it had served as a processing station for 12 million immigrants. But later in the 1950s, the General Services Administration tried to sell the island as surplus Federal property. However, no bid was high enough, and no sale was made. The doors were locked, the buildings remained empty and subject to vandals for over 10 years. With donations of private citizens who mounted a campaign to preserve the island, it was finally restored to its former grandeur and opened to the public in September of 1990.

Restoration of Ellis Island's Main Building was the most extensive of any single building in the United States. It is the fourth largest museum in New York City, exhibiting over 5000 artifacts and photographs that trace the history of the island and the poignant story of the immigrants who entered America through its golden doors.

Go On ▶

Forty-eight years after I had stepped onto Ellis Island for the first time, I paid a visit to the Ellis Island Immigration Museum. I toured the Baggage Room, and the Great Hall, and the Registry Room where I had done my best to translate questions and answers as a somewhat bewildered 14-year-old, back in 1951. I listened to some of the voices of immigrants in the Oral History Library and read many of the names listed among the 420,000 entries at the Immigrant Wall of Honor. The tour took three hours, but I lingered for five hours and had a vision of that bewildered 14-year-old girl on her way to a new life.

"It will be a good life," I told her. "You will love America."

When I finally was boarding the ferry to leave the island, I glanced back at the majestic building and at the Statue of Liberty in the backdrop, and I thanked my lucky stars that they are a part of my and my children's heritage.

13. What is the major idea of the passage?

    ○ A. It took many hours for immigrants to get processed and admitted to America.
    ○ B. The restoration of Ellis Island will help immigrants and others trace their history.
    ○ C. Most immigrants no longer enter the United States through the Port of New York.
    ○ D. It could take up to 10 harrowing days on a stormy Atlantic Ocean to reach New York Harbor.

14. What does the phrase *back in it's hey day* in paragraph seven tell about the immigration depot during the early 1900s?

    ○ A. During the 1900s, things at the immigration depot were slow and boring.
    ○ B. During the 1900s, the immigration depot was in bad shape and falling apart.
    ○ C. During the 1900s, many immigrants were being processed at the immigration depot.
    ○ D. During the 1900s, people could tour the fourth largest museum in New York City.

15. Which one of the following sentences shows a fact given in the selection?

    ○ A. On September 17, 1951, the author and her family arrived in New York Harbor.
    ○ B. Many immigrants were released to friendly looking sponsors.
    ○ C. Ellis Island is the most famous landmark in the world.
    ○ D. Everyone has family members that passed through New York Harbor.

Go On ▶

16. Which one of the following ideas can be inferred from the selection?

   ○ A. The narrator was not happy to leave her homeland.
   ○ B. The narrator was a rebellious 14-year-old girl.
   ○ C. The narrator is thankful the Ellis Island Immigration Depot was restored.
   ○ D. The narrator is sad that immigrants had to go through hard days at sea.

17. What is the author trying to make the readers feel? Does she succeed? Use details from the story to explain your answer.

   _____

   _____

   _____

18. Through whom do readers experience this story? How would the story change if it were told from a tour guide's point of view?

   _____

   _____

   _____

   _____

   _____

Directions: Read the following passage to answer questions 19 through 23.

Dorothea Lange: American Documentary Photographer
by Bethany Hansgen

On May 26, 1895, a woman was born who would forever impact modern documentary photography. Her name was Dorothea Lange. Born in Hoboken, New Jersey, Lange attended grade school in New York City's Lower East Side. As a child, Lange contracted polio, which she believed allowed her to develop the sensitivity she displayed toward others' sufferings.

From 1914 to 1917, while attending the New York Training School for Teachers, Lange met portrait photographer Arnold Genthe and became his assistant. Lange's interest in photography flourished, and, in 1917 and 1918, she attended Columbia University studying under Clarence White, a member of the group of photography called *Photo-Secession*.

Go On ▶

In 1919, Lange married painter Maynard Dixon, moved to San Francisco, California, and opened a portrait studio, which she ran until 1940. However, Lange's career had not peaked. In 1929, during the Great Depression, Lange took her camera to the streets photographing breadlines, waterfront strikes, and people suffering from the effects of the Depression. Lange remembers, "It came to me that what I had to do was concentrate on people, all kinds of people, people who paid me and people who didn't."

And, Lange did concentrate on people as seen in her photograph *White Angel Breadline* (1932), which focuses on a single destitute man standing among many other homeless men gathered around the White Angel breadline set up by a wealthy woman.

Lange's photographs attracted the attention of economist, Paul Schuster Taylor, whom she later married in 1935, the same year she was hired to work for the federal Resettlement Administration, later called the Farm Securities Administration (FSA). While working for the FSA, Lange brought the conditions of the poor to the public eye by documenting the extreme poverty of migrant workers and their families as they moved West trying to escape the Dust Bowl. In these photographs she couples hopelessness with dignity and pride, and were so effective, California established camps for migrants. During her work for the FSA, Lange photographed a migrant worker's wife surrounded by her three children. This photograph, *Migrant Mother* (1936), became an instant symbol of the migrant experience and is the most famous and most published photograph of the FSA project.

In 1941, Lange was awarded a Guggenheim Fellowship to work on a project photographing the American social scene. However, with United States entry into World War II, the U.S. War Relocation Agency hired Lange to document the relocation of Japanese-Americans to detention camps. During the war, Lange also documented the creation of United Nations in San Francisco and the women and minorities working in wartime industries in California shipyards.

Lange's health limited her from working after WWII, but in 1950, she began participating in photographic conferences. In 1954, Lange became a photographer for *Life* magazine producing many photo-essays such as *Mormon Villages* and *The Irish Countryman*.

In 1963, Lange was honored for her profound and influential photography with her acceptance to the Honor Roll of the American Society of Magazine Photographers, now the American Society of Media Photographers. She was also honored with solo exhibitions at the San Francisco Museum of Art in 1960 and the Victoria and Albert Museum in London in 1973.

Lange died of cancer on October 11, 1965, but her photographs and influence remain. One year after her death, her husband, Paul Taylor, gifted her collection to the Oakland Museum of California, and she was honored by a retrospective exhibition at the Museum of Modern Art in New York City.

Go On ▶

19. Which one of the following choices completes the time line below?

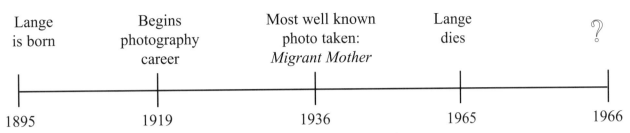

| Lange is born | Begins photography career | Most well known photo taken: *Migrant Mother* | Lange dies | ? |

1895   1919   1936   1965   1966

○ A. Lange was honored by her acceptance to the Honor Roll of the American Society of Magazine Photographers.
○ B. Lange was hired by the Farm Security Administration (FSA).
○ C. Lange's husband gifted her collection to the Oakland Museum of California.
○ D. Lange studied with Clarence White.

20. Which one of the following does the quote below imply?

Lange remembers, "It came to me that what I had to do was concentrate on people, all kinds of people, people who paid me and people who didn't."

○ A. Lange took pictures with hopes of becoming rich.
○ B. Lange photographed people during the Great Depression.
○ C. Lange was more interested in documenting people in society rather than in earning money.
○ D. Lange took pictures of people when they were young and then when they were old.

21. Why did Lange take pictures of homeless people?

○ A. She felt sorry for them.
○ B. She wanted society to pay attention to them.
○ C. She wanted to sell the pictures.
○ D. She didn't have anything to photograph.

Go On ▶

22. Why was Lange placed on the Honor Roll of the American Society of Magazine Photographers in 1963? Use evidence from the selection to support your answer.

_____

_____

_____

_____

23. Use three words to describe Dorothea Lange. Support your choices with examples from the selection.

_____

_____

_____

_____

_____

_____

STOP

Day Two

Directions: Read the following passage to answer questions 24 through 28.

Pitcher Mountain
by Karinne Heise

Once we passed the funny-looking cows, we knew we were almost there. The long-haired cows, Scottish Highlanders, grazed in a meadow fenced in by old stone walls made of New Hampshire granite. In the back seat, my two brothers and I bounced as my dad steered our old red Scout off the blacktop and onto the dirt road that took us to the top of Pitcher Mountain. A white-haired man at the entrance to the road waved to us, and my dad rolled down his window.

"How're the beh-ries this ye-ah?" Dad asked, using his fake New Hampshire accent.

"It's a good ye-ah for pickin'," answered the man, wiping his hands on the apron he used to collect money. "Head on up to numbah 10. That's whe-yah you'll find the best beh-ries."

We all waved, Mom and Dad in the black bucket seats in front and us kids in the back; the Scout spurted a bit of gravel from its tires, and up we continued on our yearly August trek to pick blueberries.

A weathered, wooden flagpole marked the parking area on top of the mountain. We clambered out of the car onto a grassy knoll surrounded by the high-bush blueberries covering the entire mountain top. Strapping coffee can containers around our waists with rope so we'd have both hands free for picking, we set off toward a path that meandered through the bushes, each in search of the best bush.

For my dad, the best bush was one near other pickers so he could eavesdrop on their conversations and then entertain us with impersonations on our drive home. My mom, efficient and eager, scouted out bushes with the largest clumps of berries, while my younger brothers tended to find bushes near the large granite boulders jutting up along the ridge line so that they could take breaks from picking for games of King of the Hill. I liked to find the bush that would set me up with the best northwestern view. The blues and greens nearby were always distinct; green leaves offset the blueberries in front of me and dark green forests surrounded the deep blue lakes in the valley below the mountain. Each layer of green hills in the distance, though, grew more faint until my eye could barely distinguish the Green Mountains in Vermont from the blue horizon of the sky.

Go On ▶

The first berries I picked plunked loudly and unsatisfyingly in my can. Each berry seemed like an effort and too small to make a difference. But once I had covered the bottom of my can, the berries dropped silently and I didn't think about what I was doing. I sneaked peeks at the mountains and listened to the buzz of the insects and the white-throated sparrows singing, "O sweet Canada Canada Canada" overhead. And every so often, I indulged in eating a handful of the sweet, juicy berries.

At the designated time, we met by the car to see who had picked the most berries and who had the bluest tongue and teeth. Mom won both competitions. It was tough to step from the cool fresh breezes of the mountain top into the hot stale air of the car, until Mom announced, "Blueberry pie for dessert tonight!" I could smell the pie the whole way home.

24. What would the narrator probably tell a friend about this family outing?

   ○ A. This trip is fun for everybody in the family because there are many things to see and do.
   ○ B. This trip is kind of fun, but she would rather go to another place next year.
   ○ C. This trip is no fun if you don't know how to make blueberry pie.
   ○ D. This is the worst place to go for a family outing because it is boring and you have to be inside all day.

25. Why does the narrator say, "the berries I picked plunked loudly and unsatisfyingly in my can"?

   ○ A. To show that the berries tasted bad.
   ○ B. To show how the task of picking berries is unrewarding.
   ○ C. To show how the sound of one berry seems too small to make a difference.
   ○ D. To show how she feels about picking berries.

26. What is the setting of this story?

   ○ A. the inside of a pick-up truck
   ○ B. a small fruit stand in the mountains
   ○ C. a mountain located in New Hampshire
   ○ D. a grassy field

Go On ▶

27. Would you have wanted to pick berries? Support your answer using evidence from the story.

_____

_____

_____

28. How does the author convey the message to readers that blueberry picking is fun for the whole family?

_____

_____

_____

Directions: Read the following passage to answer questions 29 through 34.

Solo
by Corinne Pratz

Marla took a deep breath to calm herself. It didn't help. She tried again. She held her hand out and thought the trembling had lessened.

"Ready to go, Marla?" Mr. Roberts asked her, somewhat winded. She noticed the tiny beads of perspiration on his forehead and upper lip. Obviously, he'd been running around backstage making sure everyone was prepared.

"I think so." Unconsciously, she nervously wrung her hands.

He stopped and faced her, his eyes meeting hers. "Try to relax, Marla. You know the piece. Just pretend you're in the practice room down the hall instead of on stage, OK?" He smiled warmly.

She nodded and returned his smile. Another deep breathe. She felt a little better. If Mr. Roberts was so sure she could do it, then maybe, just maybe, she could.

She smoothed her dress as she watched Tina play her piece. She sat perched atop a wooden stool alive with the exquisite flow of music that rose from tiny places where her bow connected with the violin string before connecting with another. Her arm danced, and it looked as though Tina herself was a note singing with all the others.

Go On ▶

Even though she had seen Tina play a hundred times before, Marla still became entranced. She thought she was beautiful, though she'd never actually tell her that. She doubted she looked anything like that when she played. In fact, she was almost certain she looked like one of those cardboard cutouts as she sat before the row of white and black keys.

Tina was playing the final bars to her piece. Marla was next. Suddenly, she began to shake again. She could feel her heart pounding in her chest.

She wanted to turn and run as far and as fast as she could to get away. Even though she had put off her premiere solo all year, she suddenly felt she should have put it off even longer. Maybe she just wasn't ready! Maybe she never would be ready!

Panicked, she looked around, and as her wide eyes fell upon Mr. Roberts, he held up his thumb and nodded encouragingly. Suddenly, she stopped, and in a fleeting second, she thought of her family out in the audience proudly awaiting her performance. She thought of Mr. Roberts' steady encouragement. She thought of her friends. She turned and faced the stage. She couldn't back out. Not now.

Tina had finished and was bowing to the waves of applause. Marla drew in another breath. Even if she bombed, she now felt a new determination to try.

Tina met her just behind the curtain. Derrick, the concert Master of Ceremonies was about to announce her.

"Go for it, Marla! Dazzle them." Tina exclaimed.

". . . Miss Marla Stenson." Derrick announced as he held an outstretched arm clad in a new black suit sleeve toward her.

"Go! You can do it!" Tina urged.

On legs that felt like half-cooked spaghetti noodles, she shyly stepped onto the stage and made her way to the center. She was terrified that her knees would give out as she made her introductory bow before the clapping audience. They held much to her relief. Spotlights blinded her to the audience before her, and, as she turned toward the glossy instrument, she was glad for this. She took her place on the bench. The audience grew quiet. She moved her fingers to warm them, she could hear someone cough and someone else saying, "Shhh."

Her hands felt shaky and damp, yet they felt like they had a mind of their own. They placed themselves onto the starting keys. She sat poised for a moment, and she began to play the music in her mind. Instinctively, her fingers moved to the sounds within her and the notes could be heard aloud. The more she played, one note, one key, one ping at a time, the more she forgot about the people whose ears were receiving the sounds. And before she could even think about how she was playing, she touched the final note to her solo.

Go On ▶

Softly, she placed her hands upon her lap for a moment before standing for those who would judge her. She was almost startled when the roar of applause hit her. Dumbfounded, it took her another moment to realize that they were clapping for her. For her! Marla smiled widely and bowed. She had done it! The gymnasium was booming with applause. For her!

Suddenly, Derrick was beside her placing a large bouquet of red roses wrapped in tissue paper with a beautiful bow in her arms while telling the audience that this was customary for a premiere solo. She wished that moment could last forever.

29. Why does Mr. Roberts tell Marla to pretend she is in the practice room?

    ○ A. He wants Marla to practice more.
    ○ B. He hopes she will relax.
    ○ C. He wants her to skip the performance.
    ○ D. He doesn't want her to watch the other performances.

30. What is the resolution of the story?

    ○ A. Marla can't perform her music piece because she is too nervous.
    ○ B. Tina performs better than Marla, but Marla is still glad she tried.
    ○ C. Marla overcomes her fear and delivers a wonderful music piece.
    ○ D. Marla is afraid she will perform the music piece poorly.

31. What did Marla think about as she tried to gain courage to enter the stage and perform her piece?

    ○ A. her little brother
    ○ B. she rehearsed her piece in her mind
    ○ C. the flowers she would receive if she performed well
    ○ D. her family and friends who believed in her

Go On ▶

32. In the second to last paragraph, the author describes Marla as *dumbfounded*. What does the author mean?

   ○ A. Marla is excited.
   ○ B. Marla is frightened.
   ○ C. Marla is surprised.
   ○ D. Marla is sad.

33. Explain why Mr. Roberts held up his thumb and nodded encouragingly at Marla.

   _____

   _____

   _____

34. You have to recite a poem in front of your entire seventh grade class. How do you prepare yourself, using what you learned from this story? Use details from the story to explain your answer.

   _____

   _____

   _____

Directions: Read the following passage to answer questions 35 through 37.

Bala Sharks
by Anne Watkins

   Bala sharks (*balantiocheilus melanopterus*) are not sharks at all, but they are called sharks because of their body shape and large dorsal fins. These freshwater fish are native to the waters of Thailand, Borneo, and Sumatra, where they are captured as tiny specimens to be sold for the pet trade. Also known as the tri-colored shark or silver shark, they are popular fish in the home aquarium.

   The bala shark is easily recognized by its bright silver coloration, the big, whitish fins edged in black, its large scales, and its oversized, black eyes. Their graceful, streamlined bodies make bala sharks exciting to watch as they speed around their habitat.

Go On ▶

These fish are sensitive to water quality and do best in a pH of 6.5 to 7 with water temperatures ranging from 72–82 degrees Fahrenheit. They have voracious appetites and accept most foods readily. Good quality flake foods, shrimp pellets, sinking goldfish pellets, vegetation, and the occasional feeding of live foods such as daphnia or blood worms will provide a well-rounded diet for the bala.

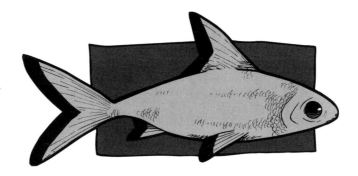

The covers on aquariums housing bala sharks must be snug fitting and secure. These fish are known to be strong jumpers and will leap out of a tank that is not tightly covered! Bala sharks, with their mild temperaments, make an excellent community fish when housed with tank mates of similar size and personality. They are non-aggressive and enjoy spending time darting from one end of the tank to the other in search of food.

Balas require large tanks to accommodate their active swimming habits. With proper care, well-maintained tank water, a good diet, and a roomy aquarium, it is possible for the quick growing bala to reach sizes of up to 13 inches in length in a home aquarium. Because they grow so rapidly, it is wise to house them in as large an aquarium as possible. A 55-gallon tank would be a good choice for the bala.

You can find these fish in almost every pet store. Most balas for sale will be very small, but sometimes larger specimens are available. Bala sharks, with their flashy silver bodies and friendly personalities, make fascinating additions to any large, home aquarium.

35. Which sentence shows an opinion given in the selection?

   ○ A. Bala sharks are exciting to watch.
   ○ B. Bala sharks are captured and sold as pets.
   ○ C. Bala sharks grow rapidly.
   ○ D. Bala sharks are not sharks at all.

36. Which detail supports the idea that bala sharks make great aquarium fish?

   ○ A. The bala shark is easily recognizable.
   ○ B. The bala shark is captured in the waters of Thailand.
   ○ C. The bala will eat live food such as daphnia or bloodworms.
   ○ D. The non-aggressive bala makes a good community fish.

Go On ▸

37. Suppose your friend would like to add a bala shark to his aquarium, what are three important tips you would share with your friend about caring for a bala? Refer to the text to tell why the tips are important.

_____

_____

_____

_____

Directions: Read the following passage to answer questions 38 through 40.

Mystery of the Pyramids
by Timothy Kevin Perry

It has been said that all the knowledge of the Earth, its past, present, and future, is contained in the Pyramids. For centuries, scientists worldwide have marveled at their strangely excellent mathematical form and symmetry. Even Sir Isaac Newton came to investigate the Pyramids. His conclusions were astounding. Along with such scientific geniuses, many other professionals have also wondered about the uncanny mysteries these structures contain. Every time an analyst uncovers another amazing mystery about them, fresh new puzzles surface right behind it. The Egyptian Pyramids were built to serve as burial grounds for kings and queens. Traditional explanation also states that the Great Pyramid, located in what is now Giza, served as the model for the others that followed it. By the various dimensions and angles they possess, some feel these structures were used as celestial star markers. Other researchers go several steps further and suggest they were star markers built and designed by ancient extra-terrestrials.

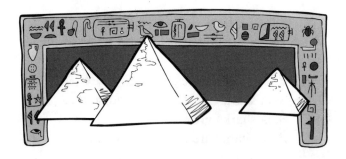

These structures can be seen as far away as the moon. The *Apollo* astronauts even commented about this fact. One wonders, why would Egyptians design objects that can be viewed from outside the Earth's atmosphere? How would they have known about things like this during an era when most everyone believed the world was still flat and humans were the only beings in a flat-headed universe?

Go On ▶

There are other uncanny aspects about these pyramids as well. Built to face true North, the Great Pyramid is located at the precise center of Earth's land, and has an East–West axis which corresponds to the longest land parallel across the planet. The Great Pyramid is thirty times larger than New York's Empire State Building. Many scientists today still can't understand how laborers working with primitive equipment could've actually placed these 15-ton stones with as much accuracy as modern machine methods. These strange, mysterious structures were built with an amazing 0.02 inch gap deliberately devised in between each stone. This arrangement allows enough space for the seal and glue to hold the stones together.

Throughout centuries, various world conquerors have been obsessed with the Pyramids and the mysterious secrets they contain. Napoleon was so fascinated with the Great Pyramid, that when his forces arrived there during the French Conquests, he deliberately spent a night inside it. It must've been a very scary night because Napoleon emerged, blanched white in shock. His experience was so devastating that he wouldn't discuss what had happened to him, with even his closest aides and officers.

Whatever is the ultimate truth behind the Pyramids, one thing can not be denied, they remain one of the most intriguing mysteries of the world.

38. Which one of the following is an opinion stated in the text?

   ○ A. These buildings can be seen as far away as the moon.
   ○ B. All knowledge is contained in the Great Pyramid.
   ○ C. The Pyramids were built with a 0.02-inch gap between each stone.
   ○ D. Napoleon was fascinated with the Great Pyramid.

39. Why does the author choose the word *obsessed* in the fourth paragraph to describe conquerors' interests in the Pyramids?

   ○ A. to show that they are nervous about the Pyramids
   ○ B. to show that they are preoccupied with the Pyramids
   ○ C. to show that they are uninterested in the Pyramids
   ○ D. to show that they are not concerned about the Pyramids

40. Which one of the following sentences is **not** true about the text?

   ○ A. The Egyptian Pyramids were built to serve as burial grounds for kings and queens.
   ○ B. Today, scientists still can't understand how laborers placed 15-ton stones without machines.
   ○ C. After spending the night in the Great Pyramid, Napoleon was delighted to share his experience.
   ○ D. The truth behind the Great Pyramid still remains an intriguing mystery.

STOP

Writing

Introduction

The Writing section of the Washington Assessment of Student Learning (WASL) is designed to measure your writing skills up to a seventh-grade level. You will be assessed on your ability to write effectively. This means you will follow writing conventions like using correct grammar and spelling. You will also make your writing interesting and show your personal style. You can do this by using sentences of different lengths and specific details to explain your ideas. To prepare for the writing assessment, practice the writing process: prewriting, writing a first draft, revising and editing your first draft, and writing a final draft. These skills are all important for effective writing.

You will take this test over two days. You will respond to one prompt on each day. Take your time to gather and organize your ideas. Use the checklists provided to help you show what you know about effective writing. Only your **final draft** will be scored in the writing assessment.

In this chapter, you will complete four practice writing assessments designed to help you practice your writing skills. Following these practice items, there two sample assessment tests, Day One and Day Two, which have been created to simulate the experience of taking the WASL Writing test.

Writing Assessment 1

Directions: If you could have the job of your dreams, what job would you choose? In several paragraphs, <u>explain</u> to your classmates what that job would be and why you would choose it.

To begin writing your essay to your classmates, you will follow the writing process: prewriting, writing a first draft, revising, editing, and writing a final draft. Use your own paper to do your prewriting and to write your final draft. **Only your final draft will be scored.**

Use the checklist below to help you write your response. Read the checklist before you begin your prewriting to help you focus on your task. Once you complete a part on the checklist, place a checkmark in that box. If, in your first draft, you leave some of the boxes on the checklist blank, revise your first draft to make your writing more effective. Read the checklist again before and after you complete your final draft to make sure your writing is effective.

✓ Checklist

My essay will be effective if I:

- [ ] follow the directions given in the writing task
- [ ] focus on the topic
- [ ] use specific and interesting details, reasons, and/or examples to support my ideas
- [ ] organize my writing with an introduction, a body, and a conclusion
- [ ] organize my writing into paragraphs
- [ ] use transitions to connect my ideas
- [ ] use language that is appropriate for my audience and purpose
- [ ] use different types and lengths of complete sentences
- [ ] use correct capitalization and punctuation
- [ ] use correct grammar
- [ ] spell words correctly

Prewriting

Directions: Use the prewriting stage to generate and record ideas to use in your paper. Choose a prewriting strategy to help you focus on the topic, audience, and purpose. The following are prewriting strategies that you may choose to use: freewriting, drawing, brainstorming, or another form of prewriting you prefer. Brainstorming includes thinking, listing, mind mapping, and clustering. **Your prewriting will not be scored.**

First Draft

Directions: Use your best prewriting ideas to write your first draft. Use scratch paper to write your first draft. You may cross out words and sentences in this draft. You may use a dictionary or thesaurus. When you have made revisions and edits to your prewriting, write your final draft. You may make any last minute revisions directly on your final draft. Read the checklist to make sure you have done your most effective writing. **Your first draft will not be scored.**

Final Draft

Remember to read the checklist on page 92 before you write your final draft. Make sure you have made all your corrections and revisions to your first draft. Write your final draft on your own paper. Fill at least the front and back of one sheet of paper. You may use more if you need to.

Once you have finished your final draft, reread the checklist to make sure your writing is effective. You may make any final corrections or revisions directly on your final draft. **Your final draft will be scored.**

Writing Assessment 2

Directions: If you knew you had the ability to have a positive impact on the students in your school, <u>explain</u>, in several paragraphs, what you would say to your peers at a school assembly.

To begin writing your speech to your peers, you will follow the writing process: prewriting, writing a first draft, revising, editing, and writing a final draft. Use your own paper to do your prewriting and to write you final draft. **Only your final draft will be scored.**

Use the checklist below to help you write your response. Read the checklist before you begin your prewriting to help you focus on your task. Once you complete a part on the checklist, place a checkmark in that box. If, in your first draft, you leave some of the boxes on the checklist blank, revise your first draft to make your writing more effective. Read the checklist again before and after you complete your final draft to make sure your writing is effective.

✔	Checklist

My speech will be effective if I:

- [ ] follow the directions given in the writing task
- [ ] focus on the topic
- [ ] use specific and interesting details, reasons, and/or examples to support my ideas
- [ ] organize my writing with an introduction, a body, and a conclusion
- [ ] organize my writing into paragraphs
- [ ] use transitions to connect my ideas
- [ ] use language that is appropriate for my audience and purpose
- [ ] use different types and lengths of complete sentences
- [ ] use correct capitalization and punctuation
- [ ] use correct grammar
- [ ] spell words correctly

Prewriting

Directions: Brainstorm some ideas about what issues you think affect students at your school. Then, list the things you might say to them about each of these issues. Choose one of the ideas that seems focused and one of the ideas which you know the most about. Use free writing, outlining, webbing, clustering, listing, or questioning strategies for effective brainstorming. Remember this is where you do your thinking and planning. **Your prewriting will not be scored.**

First Draft

Directions: Write your first draft on scratch paper. You may use a dictionary or a thesaurus. You may cross out words or sentences at this stage. After making your corrections, refer to the checklist before writing your final draft. Make any last minute revisions on your final draft. **Your first draft will not be scored.**

Final Draft

Remember to read the checklist on page 94 before you write your final draft. Make sure you have made all your corrections and revisions to your first draft. Write your final draft on your own paper. Fill at least the front and back of one sheet of paper. You may use more if you need to.

Once you have finished your final draft, reread the checklist to make sure your writing is effective. You may make any final corrections or revisions directly on your final draft. **Your final draft will be scored.**

Writing Assessment 3

Directions: You want to make the school library more comfortable. Write a letter to your principal identifying what items you would need. <u>Persuade</u> him or her and give reasons why having these items would make the library more comfortable.

To begin writing your letter to the principal, you will follow the writing process: prewriting, writing a first draft, revising, editing, and writing a final draft. Use your own paper to do your prewriting and to write your final draft. **Only your final draft will be scored.**

Use the checklist below to help you write your response. Read the checklist before you begin your prewriting to help you focus on your task. Once you complete a part on the checklist, place a checkmark in that box. If, in your first draft, you leave some of the boxes on the checklist blank, revise your first draft to make your writing more effective. Read the checklist again before and after you complete your final draft to make sure your writing is effective.

✓ Checklist

My letter will be effective if I:

- [ ] follow the directions given in the writing task
- [ ] focus on the topic
- [ ] use specific and interesting details, reasons, and/or examples to support my ideas
- [ ] organize my writing with an introduction, a body, and a conclusion
- [ ] organize my writing into paragraphs
- [ ] use transitions to connect my ideas
- [ ] use language that is appropriate for my audience and purpose
- [ ] use different types and lengths of complete sentences
- [ ] use correct capitalization and punctuation
- [ ] use correct grammar
- [ ] spell words correctly

Prewriting

Directions: Brainstorm a list of items that could make the school library more comfortable. Why are these items important? How can they make the library more comfortable? Jot down ideas for your letter. After you have finished your list, you can go back and organize your ideas. **Your prewriting will not be scored.**

First Draft

Directions: Use the best ideas from your prewriting to write your first draft. You may use a dictionary or a thesaurus. Read the checklist before writing your final draft. **Your first draft will not be scored.**

Final Draft

Remember to read the checklist on page 96 before you write your final draft. Make sure you have made all your corrections and revisions to your first draft. Write your final draft on your own paper. Fill at least the front and back of one sheet of paper. You may use more if you need to.

Once you have finished your final draft, reread the checklist to make sure your writing is effective. You may make any final corrections or revisions directly on your final draft. **Your final draft will be scored.**

Writing Assessment 4

Directions: Your school has decided to let one student choose
the lunch menu for a month. Both teachers and students will
vote on who gets to choose the lunch menu. Write a speech to
your classmates and teachers to <u>convince</u> them why you
should get to plan the lunch menu.

To begin writing your speech to your classmates and teachers, you will follow the writing process:
prewriting, writing a first draft, revising, editing, and writing a final draft. Use your own paper to do
your prewriting and to write your final draft. **Only your final draft will be scored.**

Use the checklist below to help you write your response. Read the checklist before you begin your
prewriting to help you focus on your task. Once you complete a part on the checklist, place a
checkmark in that box. If, in your first draft, you leave some of the boxes on the checklist blank, revise
your first draft to make your writing more effective. Read the checklist again before and after you
complete your final draft to make sure your writing is effective.

✓ Checklist

My speech will be effective if I:

- [ ] follow the directions given in the writing task
- [ ] focus on the topic
- [ ] use specific and interesting details, reasons, and/or examples to support my ideas
- [ ] organize my writing with an introduction, a body, and a conclusion
- [ ] organize my writing into paragraphs
- [ ] use transitions to connect my ideas
- [ ] use language that is appropriate for my audience and purpose
- [ ] use different types and lengths of complete sentences
- [ ] use correct capitalization and punctuation
- [ ] use correct grammar
- [ ] spell words correctly

Prewriting

Directions: Choose a form of brainstorming to get your ideas out onto paper. Listing, free writing, webbing, or clustering are some forms of brainstorming that may help in generating ideas. **Your prewriting will not be scored.**

First Draft

Directions: Using ideas from your prewriting activity, organize and write a draft. You may use a dictionary or a thesaurus. Revise and edit this draft before writing your final draft. Look at the checklist before you begin writing. **Your first draft will not be scored.**

Final Draft

Remember to read the checklist on page 98 before you write your final draft. Make sure you have made all your corrections and revisions to your first draft. Write your final draft on your own paper. Fill at least the front and back of one sheet of paper. You may use more if you need to.

Once you have finished your final draft, reread the checklist to make sure your writing is effective. You may make any final corrections or revisions directly on your final draft. **Your final draft will be scored.**

Writing Assessment: Day One and Day Two

Directions: The Grade 7 Washington Assessment of Student Learning for Writing will take two days. You will respond to one writing prompt each day. You will be asked to write to a persuasive prompt and an expository prompt.

Read the prompt carefully to make sure you understand what it is asking. Use the prewriting process to organize and write down your thoughts. You may choose any form of prewriting, such as webbing, listing, clustering, or a different method you prefer. Write a first draft before you write your final draft. Use this draft to make corrections and changes to your response. You can use a dictionary or a thesaurus. Read the checklist before writing your final draft.

Day One: Writing Assessment

Directions: The student store sells candy, snacks, pop, and school supplies before and after school and during lunch. Parents complained about the store being open during lunch because they felt students would not make healthy choices. The principal has ordered the store to be closed during lunch. Write a letter to the principal <u>convincing</u> him to reopen the student store.

An effective writer may consider the following points:
• Should the student store remain open during lunch?
• Should the school provide healthy food choices in the student store?
• Should the students be taught to make healthy choices?

When writing to your principal, you will follow the writing process: prewriting, writing a first draft, revising, editing, and writing a final draft. Use your own paper to do your prewriting and to write your final draft. **Only your final draft will be scored.**

Use the checklist on the next page to help you write your response. Read the checklist before you begin your prewriting to help you focus on your task. Once you complete a part on the checklist, place a checkmark in that box. If, in your first draft, you leave some of the boxes on the checklist blank, revise your first draft to make your writing more effective. Read the checklist again before and after you complete your final draft to make sure your writing is effective.

Go On ▶

✓ **Checklist**

My letter will be effective if I:

- [ ] follow the directions given in the writing task
- [ ] focus on the topic
- [ ] use specific and interesting details, reasons, and/or examples to support my ideas
- [ ] organize my writing with an introduction, a body, and a conclusion
- [ ] organize my writing into paragraphs
- [ ] use transitions to connect my ideas
- [ ] use language that is appropriate for my audience and purpose
- [ ] use different types and lengths of complete sentences
- [ ] use correct capitalization and punctuation
- [ ] use correct grammar
- [ ] spell words correctly

Prewriting

Directions: Write down some ideas for your letter to the principal. Consider the different types of prewriting activities: freewriting, webbing or clustering, listing, or another type that you prefer. **Remember, your prewriting will not be scored.**

First Draft

Directions: Make sure you read the checklist before writing your first draft. You may use a dictionary or a thesaurus. After writing the first draft, revise and edit before writing the final draft. If you need to make any final revisions or edits, make them on your final draft. **Your first draft will not be scored.**

Final Draft

Remember to read the checklist before you write your final draft. Make sure you have made all your corrections and revisions to your first draft. Write your final draft on your own paper. Fill at least the front and back of one sheet of paper. You may use more if you need to.

Once you have finished your final draft, reread the checklist to make sure your writing is effective. You may make any final corrections or revisions directly on your final draft. **Your final draft will be scored.**

STOP

Day Two: Writing Assessment

Directions: You are responsible for hosting a surprise party for your friend. In several paragraphs, <u>explain</u>, to your peers, what details are important to know about planning a surprise party. Explain why these details are important.

An effective writer may consider the following points:
• What is most important about planning a party?
• Why are these important details?

To begin your piece on the important details of hosting a surprise party, you will follow the writing process: prewriting, writing a first draft, revising, editing, and writing a final draft. Use your own paper to do your prewriting and to write your final draft. **Only your final draft will be scored.**

Use the checklist below to help you write your response. Read the checklist before you begin your prewriting to help you focus on your task. Once you complete a part on the checklist, place a checkmark in that box. If, in your first draft, you leave some of the boxes on the checklist blank, revise your first draft to make your writing more effective. Read the checklist again before and after you complete your final draft to make sure your writing is effective.

✔ Checklist

My essay will be effective if I:

- [ ] follow the directions given in the writing task
- [ ] focus on the topic
- [ ] use specific and interesting details, reasons, and/or examples to support my ideas
- [ ] organize my writing with an introduction, a body, and a conclusion
- [ ] organize my writing into paragraphs
- [ ] use transitions to connect my ideas
- [ ] use language that is appropriate for my audience and purpose
- [ ] use different types and lengths of complete sentences
- [ ] use correct capitalization and punctuation
- [ ] use correct grammar
- [ ] spell words correctly

Go On ▶

Prewriting

Directions: Jot down ideas for your party in a list. Don't worry about the order of your ideas. Before you write your first draft, you can organize your ideas. **Your prewriting will not be scored.**

First Draft

Directions: From the prewriting activity, use some of your best ideas to write your first draft. You can cross out words. You may use a dictionary or a thesaurus. Read the checklist before you begin your final draft. After writing your final draft, read the checklist to make sure you have done your most effective writing. **You first draft will not be scored.**

Final Draft

Remember to read the checklist on the previous page before you write your final draft. Make sure you have made all your corrections and revisions to your first draft. Write your final draft on your own paper. Fill at least the front and back of one sheet of paper. You may use more if you need to.

Once you have finished your final draft, reread the checklist to make sure your writing is effective. You may make any final corrections or revisions directly on your final draft. **Your final draft will be scored.**

STOP

Mathematics

Introduction

In the Mathematics section of the Washington Assessment of Student Learning (WASL), you will be asked questions designed to gauge the knowledge you have gained thus far in your academic career. These questions have been constructed based on the mathematical skills you have been taught in school through seventh grade. The questions you answer are not meant to confuse or trick you, but are written so that you have the best opportunity to show what you know® about mathematics.

Within this portion of the WASL, you will be faced with a variety of question formats including multiple-choice, short-answer, extended multiple-choice (scored as short-answer questions), and extended-response. These different question formats will allow you to demonstrate your knowledge in many different ways, including through numbers, words, pictures, graphs, and charts.

You will complete 60 practice items designed to help you practice your test-taking skills. Following these practice items, there are two sample assessment tests, Day One and Day Two, which have been created to simulate the experience of taking the WASL Mathematics test. A glossary of mathematics terms used on the WASL has been included at the end of this chapter for your reference. This glossary is only a study tool and cannot be used while answering either the practice items or the questions on the sample assessment tests.

Practice Items

1. For a cooking unit in class, Josh had to line up his measuring spoons from **smallest** to **largest**. What is the correct order?

   ○ A. $\frac{1}{4}$ tsp., $\frac{1}{8}$ tsp., $\frac{1}{2}$ tsp., 1 tsp.

   ○ B. $\frac{1}{8}$ tsp., $\frac{1}{4}$ tsp., $\frac{1}{2}$ tsp., 1 tsp.

   ○ C. $\frac{1}{8}$ tsp., $\frac{1}{2}$ tsp., $\frac{1}{4}$ tsp., 1 tsp.

   ○ D. 1 tsp., $\frac{1}{2}$ tsp., $\frac{1}{4}$ tsp., $\frac{1}{8}$ tsp.

2. Rick's batting average is .450. Jed's batting average is .356. Dave's batting average is .540. Brad's batting average is .347. Choose the correct order of batting averages from **greatest** to **least**.

   ○ A. .450, .540, .356, .347
   ○ B. .347, .356, .450, .540
   ○ C. .540, .450, .356, .347
   ○ D. .540, .450, .347, .356

3. Which expression equals the number 12 written as a product of its prime factors?

   ○ A. 2 x 2 x 3
   ○ B. 1 x 2 x 3 x 4
   ○ C. 4 x 3
   ○ D. 6 x 2

4. Mrs. Ming's math extra credit problems require solving for mystery numbers. Solve the mystery: I am the largest possible factor of 32 **and** 6. What number am I?

   ○ A. 1
   ○ B. 2
   ○ C. 3
   ○ D. 4

5. In which of the following equations is multiplication **not** the first step?

    ○ A. $5 \times 10 + 3 = n$
    ○ B. $7 - (3 \times 2) = n$
    ○ C. $6 + 3(4 + 2) = n$
    ○ D. $2[(6 \times 3) + 4 - 10] = n$

6. In the equation $n = 3(y + 3) + 2$, the value of y is 3. Which of the following should be done first to solve for n?

    ○ A. multiply 6 by 3
    ○ B. add $3 + 3$
    ○ C. multiply 3 by 3
    ○ D. add $6 + 2$

7. The local zoo charges $1.99 for admission. If they have 20,761 visitors in one week, estimate the average amount of money made from admission per day. Compare your estimation to the exact computation, and decide if the estimation is good.

    _____

    _____

8. In order to play baseball, each player must average $1,500.00 in donations. Eight ball players have turned in a total of $10,476.59. Estimate how much money the ninth ball player needs to collect in order for the team to meet their goal for donations. **Explain your answer in detail.**

    _____

    _____

    _____

9. Stacy, Rick, and Keith shared a pizza. Stacy ate one-fourth of the pizza, Rick ate one-third of the pizza, and Keith ate five-twelfths of the pizza. Who ate the most pizza?

    ○ A. Stacy
    ○ B. Keith
    ○ C. Rick
    ○ D. They all ate the same amount.

10. The Seattle Sailors are giving out free tickets to students in the King County area. Three-fifths of all middle school students receive a ticket. What percent of the students do **not** receive a ticket?

    _____

11. Mark has 3 CDs, 6 trading cards, 2 books, and 1 candy bar. What is the ratio of CDs to books? What is the ratio of CDs to the total number of objects?

    _____

12. In the city, there are three cars to one parking space. How many parking spaces would there be for 5 times as many cars?

    ○ A. 2 parking spaces
    ○ B. 15 parking spaces
    ○ C. 3 parking spaces
    ○ D. 5 parking spaces

13. Sally is having a garage sale. She needs space for 5 boxes. The base of each box measures 3' x 2'. Each tabletop she has measures 4' x 7'. How many tables will she use to fit the boxes on? **Note: A box must fit completely on a table.**

    ○ A. 1 table
    ○ B. 2 tables
    ○ C. 3 tables
    ○ D. 4 tables

14. The temperature in the swimming pool has steadily risen since 8 a.m. Create a graph in the space provided on the next page using the information in the table below to show the hourly temperature change and tell what the temperature will be at 2 p.m.

Time	Pool Temp.
8 a.m.	50°F
9 a.m.	53°F
10 a.m.	57°F
11 a.m.	62°F
12 p.m.	68°F
1 p.m.	75°F

15. Cody wants to buy a book about baseball for $18.75. His mother asks him to purchase a book on gardening which costs $16.10 and a cookbook for $14.50. Sales tax is 9.5%. Approximate how much money Cody will need to take with him to purchase all three books.

    _____

    _____

16. For a banquet, Al needs to place 6 tables end to end. Each table is 4 feet, 3 inches long. Approximate the total length of the tables.

    ○ A. 24 feet
    ○ B. 30 feet
    ○ C. 10 feet
    ○ D. 36 feet

    Is this a good situation for Al to approximate the length of six tables? **Explain your answer in detail.**

    _____

    _____

17. A builder wants to create a park on an empty lot. The lot's dimensions are 20 ft. by 40 ft. The builder wants to leave enough space within the perimeter of the park for a bike path, which is 3 ft. wide. What is the area of the park upon completion? **Explain your answer in detail.**

40 feet

20 feet

_____

_____

_____

18. Luke and his mother are making 2 gallons of homemade jelly and putting it into 8-ounce jars to store for the coming winter. How many jars can they fill? **Use the following information to solve this problem: 8 ounces = 1 cup; 2 cups = 1 pint; 2 pints = 1 quart; 4 quarts = 1 gallon.**

_____

19. Gina is in charge of timing runners in races during gym class. What can she do to record the **most precise** measure of time?

   ○ A. count to herself
   ○ B. use a clock on the wall
   ○ C. use a stopwatch
   ○ D. have the runners count out loud as they run

20. Draw a square with an area of 4 sq. in.

21. There are three different geometric terms to describe the figure below. Choose the list that has all three names for the shape.

- ○ A. square, rhombus, parallelogram
- ○ B. trapezoid, rhombus, parallelogram
- ○ C. hexagon, rhombus, parallelogram
- ○ D. square, rhombus, trapezoid

22. Look at the picture below and name at least four geometric figures you see.

_____

_____

_____

23. In the grid below, move triangle CDE four units to the right. Write the new coordinates of each vertex of the translated triangle.

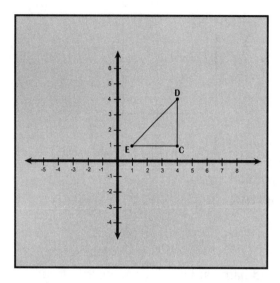

_____

_____

24. Nicco's parents asked him to plot out his new paper route on a grid. He will begin on the corner with coordinates (4, 3). He will go north until he reaches (4, 9). At that point, he will turn right and go to (12, 9) where he'll turn south and go to (12, 4). The last turn will take him back to his starting point. Show the paper route by plotting and connecting the points in the order given.

25. If triangle ABC is **similar** to triangle DEF, what is the measurement of angle DEF?

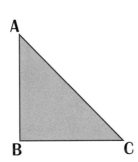
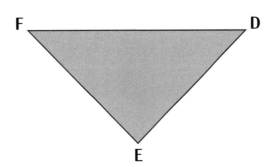

○ A. 45°
○ B. 90°
○ C. 12°
○ D. 56°

26. How many lines of symmetry does a square have?

○ A. 2 lines of symmetry
○ B. 3 lines of symmetry
○ C. 4 lines of symmetry
○ D. 6 lines of symmetry

27. Lauren spins the spinner below. The area of section 3 equals the area of section 4. The area of section 5 is twice the area of section 4. The area of section 6 equals the area of section 5. What is the probability that Lauren will spin a 6?

○ A. $\frac{1}{6}$

○ B. $\frac{1}{5}$

○ C. $\frac{2}{4}$

○ D. $\frac{1}{3}$

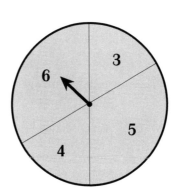

28. Each month, students with perfect attendance put their names into a bowl. The principal draws one name and gives that student a prize. If there are 16 girls and 12 boys in the drawing, what is the probability that the name drawn will be a girl's name?

    ○ A. $\dfrac{4}{3}$

    ○ B. $\dfrac{3}{4}$

    ○ C. $\dfrac{3}{7}$

    ○ D. $\dfrac{4}{7}$

29. During a canned food drive, Bethany charts the number of cans collected for each day of the week from three classes. With the following data, create a graph on the next page that Bethany might use to present information representing the total number of cans collected by each class.

    Mr. Stott's class collected the following amount of cans:
    Mon. 10 cans; Tues. 6 cans; Wed. 7 cans; Thurs. 4 cans; Fri. 9 cans.

    Mrs. Greggor's class collected the following amount of cans:
    Mon. 7 cans; Tues. 6 cans; Wed. 3 cans; Thurs. 5 cans; Fri. 7 cans.

    Mr. Bell's class collected the following amount of cans:
    Mon. 7 cans; Tues. 15 cans; Wed. 21 cans; Thurs. 3 cans; Fri. 2 cans.

30. The baseball and softball teams are collecting sponsors to advertise for their new baseball diamond. Use the information, which represents the number of sponsors collected by each team per week, from the chart below to construct a double line graph on a grid.

Week	Baseball	Softball
1	15	10
2	20	15
3	10	5
4	5	10

31. During the basketball tournament, Lisa charts the amount of candy bars sold at the concession stand. Lisa argues that the mean and median amounts of candy bars sold are equal. Is Lisa correct? **Explain your answer in detail.**

Game	Candy Bars
1	30
2	35
3	56
4	41
5	43

32. Looking at the graph below, determine the mode of the temperatures recorded for the month of May.

May Temperatures

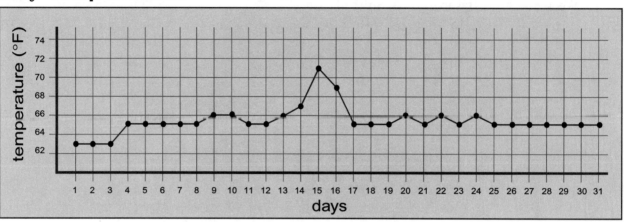

_____

_____

33. Given recent sales, Jana believes that the average price of baseball cards will triple in the next three months. John believes that the price of baseball cards will remain constant. **Use the data given and explain in detail how either person may be correct.**

Average Baseball Card Sales by Month

Month	Price
Jan.	$5.00
Feb.	$10.00
Mar.	$15.00
Apr.	$15.00
May	$15.00
Jun.	$20.00

_____

_____

_____

_____

34. Looking at the pictograph below, predict which business will have the highest number of sales.

Internet Business Activity

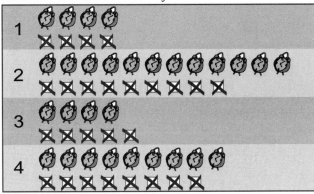

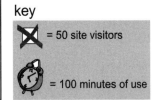

key

⊠ = 50 site visitors

🕐 = 100 minutes of use

○ A. Business 1
○ B. Business 2
○ C. Business 3
○ D. Business 4

35. A department store clerk arranged four shelves of shirts in a pyramid of colors. On the bottom level, the clerk arranged blue, black, beige, and red shirts. On the next level, black, beige, and red shirts were arranged. On the third level from the bottom, there were beige and red shirts. Following this pattern, what should be the color of the shirts on the top of the pyramid?

○ A. black
○ B. blue
○ C. red
○ D. beige

36. A sequence of dot patterns is given below. What is the next number of dots in this sequence?

• •   • • • •   • • • •
• •   • • • •   • • • •
                     • • • •
                     • • • •

○ A. 24
○ B. 32
○ C. 40
○ D. 30

37. In the equation $y = 2n + 2$, how does the value of **y** change when the value of **n** increases by 3?

   ○ A. y increases by 3
   ○ B. y decreases by 3
   ○ C. y decreases by 6
   ○ D. y increases by 6

38. Looking at Graph P, what is the correct equation for the value of **y**?

   ○ A. $y = x + 2$
   ○ B. $y = 2x + 1$
   ○ C. $y = x - 2$
   ○ D. $y = 2x - 1$

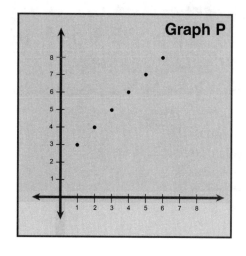

39. For which value of **n** is the equation below true?

$$3(n - 4) + 3 = 6$$

   ○ A. 1
   ○ B. 4
   ○ C. 5
   ○ D. 7

40. Antonio wants to go skating with his mother, father, brother, and sister. For one person to skate, the price is $2.00, but for the family rate, each additional person costs only $1.00. Below, write an equation that represents the family skate rate, and solve for the total cost of Antonio's family to go skating.

41. Charlotte rides her bike 5 miles one way to the gym everyday. One day a week, she rides her bike an hour longer than usual. On Tuesdays, she stays at the gym longer than on the other days and runs laps. What other piece of information is needed to determine how far Charlotte rides her bike each week?

_____

_____

42. Sergio has five classes before lunch. He has history, English, biology, math, and computer class. English comes after biology, but before history. He goes right to lunch after computer class. He is always late to math class from English. What is Sergio's schedule before lunch?

○ A. biology, English, math, history, computer
○ B. English, biology, math, history, computer
○ C. math, biology, history, computer, English
○ D. English, math, biology, history, computer

43. State the problem that the two boys must solve and the information they need to obtain in order to solve it.

Frank and Leo had a bet for the month of January. Frank said there would be 5 days or less that the temperature would drop below zero. Leo claimed the temperature would drop below zero more than 5 days. It is now February 1. How can they determine who wins the bet?

_____

_____

_____

_____

44. Javier was making a batch of brownies for a school bake sale. He accidentally doubled the amount of cocoa required. What is his problem, and how can he solve it?

○ A. Javier needs to correct his mistake by adding more of every other ingredient.
○ B. Javier needs to correct his mistake by adding less of every other ingredient.
○ C. Javier needs to correct his mistake, but it is not known how he can do this.
○ D. Javier needs to make a batch of brownies for school, but he is not a good cook.

45. Sara spent half her baby-sitting money on a new dress. With the remaining money, she bought tickets to the movies for a friend and herself, which amounted to $10.00, which was one half the amount of her remaining cash after she bought the dress. How much money did Sarah earn baby-sitting? How much money was the dress, and how much remained? **Explain, in detail, how you arrive at your answer and show your mathematical work.**

_____

_____

_____

46. Jaycee wants to buy a new bicycle for $199.00. The sales tax is 10% of the total. How much money does Jaycee need if she also plans on buying accessories that amount to $49.00? Round your answer to the nearest ten.

○ A. $210.00
○ B. $270.00
○ C. $280.00
○ D. $250.00

47. Mr. Biazzi's class is having an ice cream party. Before he went to buy the ice cream, he took a poll of the students' favorite ice cream flavors. When Mr. Biazzi arrived at the grocery store, he noticed that the vanilla ice cream was on sale for $3.99 a half-gallon. The chocolate ice cream was priced at $5.99 a half-gallon. Mr. Biazzi needs to buy 3 half-gallons for the 12 boys and 24 girls in his class. Given the information on the next page, what should Mr. Biazzi buy?

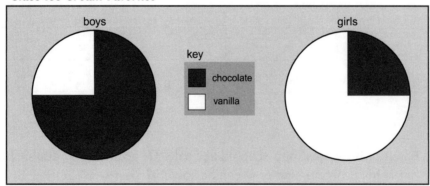

Class Ice Cream Favorites

○ A. 1 vanilla half-gallon and 1 chocolate half-gallon
○ B. 2 vanilla half-gallons and 1 chocolate half-gallon
○ C. 1 vanilla half-gallon and 2 chocolate half-gallons
○ D. 2 vanilla half-gallons and 2 chocolate half-gallons

48. Use the charts below to determine how many women in Townsville like Thanksgiving best.

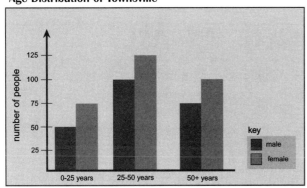

Age Distribution of Townsville

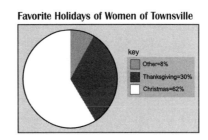

Favorite Holidays of Women of Townsville

key
Other=8%
Thanksgiving=30%
Christmas=62%

- ○ A. 30 women
- ○ B. 60 women
- ○ C. 90 women
- ○ D. 300 women

49. Jerome has a spinner that is divided into several different colored sections. Jerome uses the spinner to play his favorite board game. During one game, he spun 24 times. He spun red a total of 4 times, blue a total of 3 times, yellow a total of 4 times, and green a total of 5 times. Think about Jerome's remaining spins. Predict how many colors are **most likely** on the spinner. **Note: Each color appears only once on the spinner, and each colored section on the spinner is equal in size.**

- ○ A. 2 sections
- ○ B. 4 sections
- ○ C. 6 sections
- ○ D. 16 sections

50. Sarah, Allison, and Kristin decide to see who can blow the biggest bubble. The results of the first three trials are shown below.

Name	Trial 1	Trial 2	Trial 3
Sarah	6 in.	7 in.	8 in.
Allison	7 in.	7 in.	7 in.
Kristin	8 in.	7 in.	6 in.

Describe the trends in the trials shown and use them to predict who will blow the biggest bubble in Trial 4.

_____

_____

_____

_____

51. Stuart and Isabel have $43.00 total. Isabel has $3.00 more than 3 times the amount Stuart has saved. Will Stuart have enough money to go ice skating if the cost to go ice skating is $12.00? **Explain your answer in detail.**

_____

_____

52. The ice cream store carries only five flavors: peppermint, chocolate, strawberry, vanilla, and mocha almond fudge. Ben and his friends order only one flavor each, and each flavor is ordered at least once. Ben doesn't like chocolate; Pam doesn't like peppermint or chocolate. If Sue orders vanilla and Larry orders strawberry, what flavor will Charlotte order?

○ A. chocolate
○ B. peppermint
○ C. strawberry
○ D. mocha almond fudge

53. Looking at the diagram below, what mathematical description of the information given could you use to represent the data with a true statement?

Population Growth by Month

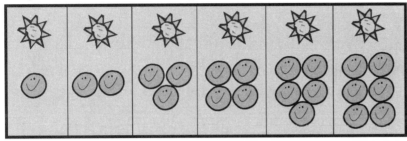

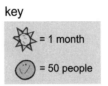

key

= 1 month

= 50 people

- ○ A. The population grows by 20 people each month.
- ○ B. The diagram displays information for a year.
- ○ C. The population grows by 50 people each month.
- ○ D. The final population is an odd number.

54. Susie is not feeling well. Read the thermometer and choose the statement that **best** describes Susie's temperature.

Temperature (°F)

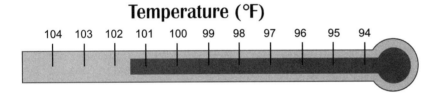

- ○ A. The thermometer reads 98.6°F.
- ○ B. The thermometer reads 101.6°F.
- ○ C. The thermometer reads 100.6°F.
- ○ D. The thermometer is not showing a temperature.

55. Jake is driving 1,500 miles across the country in his new car. He doesn't know how much money he'll need to budget for gas. When he calls the car dealership they send him the following information about his car:

tank size   13 gallons
miles/gallon   15 miles/gallon

Describe what Jake needs to do with the information on the pamphlet to plan a budget for gas, given that gas is $2.00 a gallon. How much money will Jake need for his trip?

_____

_____

_____

_____

_____

_____

56. Five friends are going to split 3 jumbo size candy bars. How can they divide the candy bars so that each person is given an equal amount of pieces? Choose the mathematical statement that best fits the solution.

○ A. The five friends can divide each candy bar into fifths.
○ B. The five friends can divide each candy bar into halves.
○ C. The five friends can divide each candy bar into thirds.
○ D. The five friends can divide each candy bar into quarters.

57. Every spring, melting snow creates a run-off of water that goes into a large reservoir. If the reservoir rises three-fourths of a foot every one-half week, how many feet will it rise in three and a half weeks?

○ A. 5 feet
○ B. 5.25 feet
○ C. 4.75 feet
○ D. 5.5 feet

58. Rudy does yard work and charges $14.00 per hour. After paying $20.50 for lawn mower gasoline one week, his remaining earnings were $179.00. How many hours did he work that week?

    ○ A. 16 hours
    ○ B. 14.5 hours
    ○ C. 14.25 hours
    ○ D. 15 hours

59. Mario and Claudine baked a pie. Mario ate one-fourth of the pie. Claudine ate 20%. What percent of the pie is left? Make a chart representing this information.

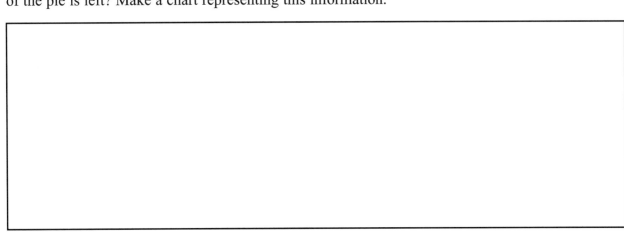

60. The figure below is a rhombus. The line (diagonal) drawn divides the rhombus into two equilateral triangles. Using this information, find the perimeter of the rhombus.

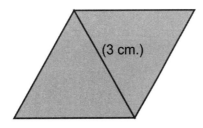

(3 cm.)

_____

What is the proportion of the length of the diagonal shown to the length of the perimeter of the rhombus?

_____

Mathematics Assessment:
Day One and Day Two

Directions: The Grade 7 Washington Assessment of Student Learning for Mathematics will take two days. On Day One of the Mathematics Assessment, you are permitted to use tools such as rulers, protractors, and calculators. On Day Two, these tools will not be permitted. There will be four types of questions for this section of the WASL. You will answer multiple-choice questions in which you pick the best answer out of four answer choices. You will fill in the circle in front of your answer choice. You will answer extended multiple-choice questions in which you pick the best answer out of four choices and then support your answer. Short-answer and extended-response questions will also be asked. These questions ask you to use words, pictures, or numbers for your response.

Read each question carefully and answer it to the best of your ability. If you do not know an answer, you may skip the question and come back to it later. Show as much of your mathematical work as possible. For short-answer and extended-response questions include many details and a thorough explanation. When you are required to write an answer, do so neatly and legibly in the space provided. Figures and diagrams with given lengths and/or dimensions may not be drawn to scale. Angle measures should be assumed to be accurate. Do not turn the page when you see the word **STOP.** When you finish, check your answers; you have have as much time as you need to complete the test. Do not look ahead or go back to another day's test.

Day One

1. Mark and Rick are looking at CDs. Rick says, "If I buy this CD and two more, I'll have a total of 14." Mark says, "If I buy this CD and 4 more, I'll have a total of 19 CDs." How many CDs does Mark have to **begin** with?

   ○ A. 15 CDs
   ○ B. 14 CDs
   ○ C. 13 CDs
   ○ D. 12 CDs

2. Marie cut 3 inches off her skirt. If **L** is the length of Marie's skirt before she cut it, and **C** is the length of her skirt now, which equation can be applied to find the length of her skirt **now**?

   ○ A. $C - L = 3$
   ○ B. $C = 3 + L$
   ○ C. $L = C - 3$
   ○ D. $C = L - 3$

3. Brian, Rob, Jim, Steve, and Pete play in a one-on-one basketball tournament. If each of them plays one game with each of the others, how many games will be played in all?

   _____

   _____

4. Billie has a bag of peanuts. She gives $\frac{1}{2}$ of them to her brother, then gets 10 more from her sister. She now has 25. Which statement below is true?

   ○ A. Billie has more peanuts than when she started.
   ○ B. Billie has the same amount of peanuts as when she started.
   ○ C. Billie gave 10 peanuts to her brother.
   ○ D. Billie has fewer peanuts than when she started.

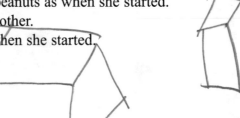

Go On ▶

5. Rich and Nynetta are doing a puzzle. Rich completed three-fifths of the puzzle, while Nynetta finished 30% of it. What percent of the puzzle have they completed?

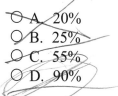

- A. 20%
- B. 25%
- C. 55%
- D. 90%

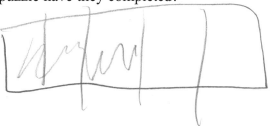

6. A total of 1,273 people had box seats at a football game. If there were 1,642 total box seats, estimate how many seats were empty.

_____

_____

7. There are 1,756 employees at an energy plant. Each employee works 42 hours a week. What is the total number of hours worked by these employees in 2 weeks?

_____

8. Main Street extends 400.4 yards. One side of Main Street is taken up entirely by four districts: Antique Alley, the Historical Section, the Super Mall, and the Amusement Park. If each of these districts takes up the same length, what is the correct operation to determine the length of each section (*n*)?

- A. $n = 3 \times 4 + 10$

- B. $\dfrac{400.4}{4} = n$

- C. $n = 400.4 - 4$

- D. $4 \times 400.4 = n$

9. How does the area of a rectangle change when the length of each side doubles?

- A. The area of the new rectangle is 2 times larger.
- B. The area of the new rectangle is 3 times larger.
- C. The area of the new rectangle is 4 times larger.
- D. The area of the new rectangle is 8 times larger.

Go On ▶

10. John told his sister she could have $\frac{2}{8}$ of the pizza, but she cut the pizza into 4 equal slices. How many slices can she eat? Using, words, numbers, charts, or pictures, show your reasoning.

_____

11. Mac sold 21 candy bars. Frank sold 32 candy bars. If a box holds 12 candy bars, how many boxes were opened?

   ○ A. 4 boxes
   ○ B. 5 boxes
   ○ C. 6 boxes
   ○ D. 53 boxes

12. Luke wants to know how far he can run in one hour. What unit of measurement will he **most likely** use to record this?

   ○ A. centimeters
   ○ B. inches
   ○ C. miles
   ○ D. minutes

13. In which expression is addition the **first** operation that should be performed?

   ○ A. 17 + 1 – 3(4 x 2)
   ○ B. 14 – 2(3 + 2)
   ○ C. 4 + 3 x 7
   ○ D. (3 x 4) – (2 + 4)

14. For any equilateral figure, what is the ratio of its number of sides to the number of lines of symmetry that can be drawn through it? Demonstrate your finding by using diagrams.

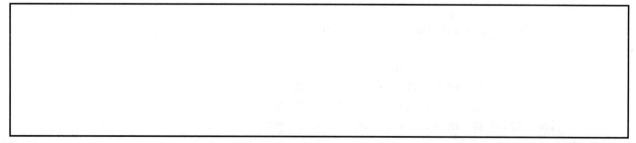

Go On ▶

15. A shirt has an original price of $32.00 before tax. Sales tax is 8% of the original price. Is it less expensive to buy the shirt at 25% off the original price, or is it less expensive to have 20% taken off the total bill after the tax is added on to the original price?

_____

_____

16. Dance class lasts 1.5 hours. An equal amount of time is spent on sit-ups, leg lifts, and dancing. How much time is spent on each activity?

○ A. 40 min.
○ B. 30 min.
○ C. 20 min.
○ D. 45 min.

17. Four students in Mrs. Picci's class are absent. They represent $\frac{1}{6}$ of the entire class. Which

equation could be used to determine the total number of students in Mrs. Picci's class where, **n** is

the total number of kids in class?

○ A. $2 \times \frac{1}{6} = n$

○ B. $4 - \frac{1}{6} = n$

○ C. $\frac{1}{6} \times \frac{1}{3} = n$

○ D. $\frac{1}{6} = \frac{4}{n}$

18. The pep club is selling buttons and seat cushions. Buttons sell for $2.50; seat cushions sell for $4.00. Friday night, the pep club sold 8 items and took in a total of $24.50. How many buttons and seat cushions did they sell? Using, words, numbers, charts, or pictures, show your reasoning.

_____

_____

Go On ▶

19. Mrs. Molyet's class decided to see how fast their hamster Moose could run through a maze. In five attempts, Moose completed the maze in the following times, recorded in seconds: 7.2, 4.4, 8.0, 6.7, and 5.2. What is the mean time of Moose's attempts?

   ○ A. 8.0 seconds
   ○ B. 6.3 seconds
   ○ C. 6.7 seconds
   ○ D. 4.4 seconds

20. Moira spins the spinner below. What is the probability that Moira will spin a 12?

   ○ A. $\dfrac{1}{4}$

   ○ B. $\dfrac{1}{2}$

   ○ C. $\dfrac{1}{8}$

   ○ D. $\dfrac{1}{12}$

Go On ▶

21. What is the area of the rhombus ABCD when segment AB = 5 inches and segment BE = 4.3 inches? **Note:** $A = b \times h$

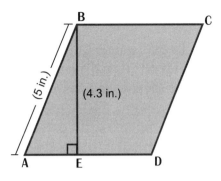

- ○ A. 21.5 sq. in.
- ○ B. 25 sq. in.
- ○ C. 20 sq. in.
- ○ D. 9.3 sq. in.

22. Given the following information, find a set of **11 numbers** that fit the data below. Then, graph the data.

Range: 5 to 15
Median: 8
Mode: 7
Mean: 9
The average of the greatest two numbers is 14.

23. Malika gave Ronnie a quarter, 3 dimes, a nickel, and two pennies, after which she had $3.00 left. How much money did she have to **begin** with?

- ○ A. $3.72
- ○ B. $2.62
- ○ C. $3.42
- ○ D. $3.62

STOP

Day Two

24. Suki and her brother went to the football game. At the game, she bought a soda for $1.50, a bag of popcorn for $1.00, a licorice rope for $0.50, and a candy bar for $1.00. If she gave $10.00 to the cashier how much money in change should she receive?

   ○ A. $5.00
   ○ B. $6.00
   ○ C. $4.50
   ○ D. $7.00

25. Movie tickets are $\frac{1}{3}$ the cost of concert tickets. If Sam spent 28 dollars on both a movie ticket and concert ticket, how much money did he spend on each? Setup and solve an equation.

   _____

   _____

26. What value of n makes the following equation true?

   $$13 - 3(n + 4) + 2 = 0$$

   ○ A. 0
   ○ B. 2
   ○ C. 1
   ○ D. 3

27. Planet X is 18,963.947 miles away from Planet M. Planet Y is 16,879.998 miles away from Planet M. Planet Y is how much closer to Planet M than Planet X?

   ○ A. 1,083.949 miles
   ○ B. 2,016.151 miles
   ○ C. 2,083.949 miles
   ○ D. 35,843.945 miles

Go On ▶

28. Rueben can run 1 lap in a minute. If 8 laps = 1 mile, when Rueben ran for 30 minutes how many miles did he run?

    ○ A. 3 $\frac{3}{4}$ miles

    ○ B. 4 $\frac{1}{4}$ miles

    ○ C. 3 miles

    ○ D. 4 miles

29. Doug wants to visit his grandmother. There are two bus routes which go directly from his town to his grandmother's town, with no stops in between. Assuming the buses always go the speed limit, which route should Doug travel to get to his grandmother's house in the least amount of time? **Explain your answer in detail.**

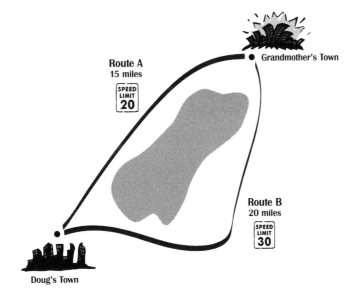

Route A
15 miles
SPEED LIMIT 20

Grandmother's Town

Route B
20 miles
SPEED LIMIT 30

Doug's Town

_____

_____

_____

_____

30. What percent of the semi-circle below is shaded?

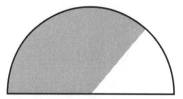

- ○ A. 33%
- ○ B. 40%
- ○ C. 66%
- ○ D. 50%

31. Of the 23 students who signed up for Drama Club, eight are boys. What is the fraction of girls who signed up for the club?

- ○ A. $\dfrac{7}{23}$

- ○ B. $\dfrac{15}{23}$

- ○ C. $\dfrac{23}{15}$

- ○ D. $\dfrac{8}{15}$

32. The length of the side of the square below has been rounded to the nearest inch. What is the **smallest** perimeter the square may actually have? (Note: drawing not to scale.)

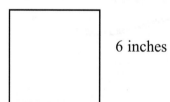

6 inches

- ○ A. 36 inches
- ○ B. 25 inches
- ○ C. 24 inches
- ○ D. 22 inches

Go On ▶

33. If you were to shade $\frac{1}{4}$ of the figure below, how many squares would you shade?

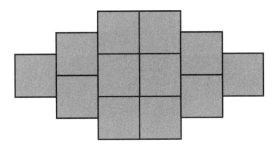

- ○ A. 3 squares
- ○ B. 4 squares
- ○ C. 6 squares
- ○ D. 8 squares

34. If triangle ABC is **similar** to triangle DEF, what is the length of DE?

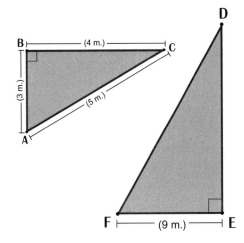

_____

_____

35. Jeff flies an airplane. When he flies weekdays, he earns $100.00 a day. When he flies weekends, he earns $200.00 a day. If Jeff flew a total of 5 days during a two-week period, and he earned a total of $500.00, is it possible to determine how many weekdays he flew? Why or why not?

_____

_____

Go On ▶

36. Elizabeth flips a penny 50 times in a row and gets heads each time, what is the probability that she will get heads the next time she flips the penny?

   ○ A. 1:2
   ○ B. 1:50
   ○ C. 1:51
   ○ D. 2:1

37. A box of 48 chocolates has $\frac{1}{4}$ caramel, 50% cream filled, and $\frac{2}{8}$ with nuts. Make a bar graph showing the box of candy with given amounts shown.

38. The number 42 is a multiple of what number?

   ○ A. 5
   ○ B. 4
   ○ C. 3
   ○ D. 8

39. Selma gets paid a base of $10.00 a day, plus $5.00 for every hour she baby-sits. If she made $35.00 last Friday, how many hours did she baby-sit?

   ○ A. 4 hours
   ○ B. 7 hours
   ○ C. 6 hours
   ○ D. 5 hours

Go On ▶

40. Lauren is decorating a 6" by 7" by 4" rectangular box in which to put her valentines. She wants to glue ribbon around the top edge. How many inches of ribbon does she need?

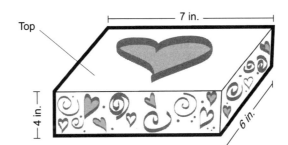

Top

7 in.

4 in.

6 in.

- ○ A. 17 in.
- ○ B. 26 in.
- ○ C. 42 in.
- ○ D. 168 in.

41. During math class, Mrs. Cramer asked her students to estimate how full the peanut jar was. Steven estimated the jar was $\frac{3}{5}$ full. Kristi estimated the jar to be 50% full. Mrs. Cramer said both responses were wrong, but the correct answer is between the two guesses. Choose a percent that could be **possible**.

- ○ A. 50%
- ○ B. 55%
- ○ C. 60%
- ○ D. 35%

42. Stanley is saving money to buy a plane ticket. The ticket costs $500.00. He already has saved $263.00. Every week, he earns an $8 allowance and $15 mowing lawns. If he saves all the money he earns, how many more weeks will it take for him to earn enough to buy the ticket?

_____

_____

43. If Ruby is to continue the pattern, what is the **next** number?

        1   5   13   29   ____

- ○ A. 58
- ○ B. 61
- ○ C. 42
- ○ D. 32

Go On ▶

44. Sue and Beth drive in the carpool lane 45.5% of the way to work. Sue rides alone 33% of the way. Approximately, by rounding to the nearest ten percent, what portion of the route is not accounted for.

    ○ A. 20%
    ○ B. 30%
    ○ C. 40%
    ○ D. 21.5%

45. Serretta is making a flag following the proportions in the pattern given below. For her flag, she is using 1.5 yards of fabric for the shaded section. What is the ratio of the shaded area to the area of the entire flag?

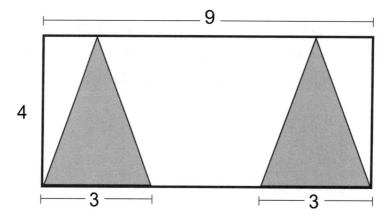

    ○ A. 1:3
    ○ B. 3:10
    ○ C. 3:1
    ○ D. 1:2

    How much fabric does she need for the non-shaded area?

    _____

    _____

46. Jake is building a bird feeder. The base of the bird feeder is a 4" by 4" square. The top of the birdfeeder is congruent to the base. He plans to use 4 rectangular pieces of wood for the body of the feeder that are 7 inches high. How much wood will Jake need to build the entire bird feeder?

    _____

    _____

    _____

STOP

Glossary of Terms on the 7th Grade WASL in Mathematics

Accuracy – How close to the actual value a number is; the closer a value is to the actual value, the more accurate it is. Consider the following example, based on a dartboard. Suppose you are trying to hit the number 20 at the top of the board. You throw three darts, one of which hits the number 1 (which is directly to the right of the number 20), another hits the bull's-eye (which is directly below the number 20), and the other hits the number 5 (which is directly to the left of the number 20). Although the darts never hit the intended target, the throws are relatively close to the target, and, therefore, relatively accurate. (see **Precision**)

Acute – An **angle** with a measure less than 90°.

Angle – The distance, recorded in degrees (°), between two **segments** which meet at a common **vertex**. Angles can be **obtuse**, **acute**, or **right**. A straight line is considered to be an angle of 180°.

Approximate – To obtain an answer that is not necessarily exact, but close enough for the given situation. An example of a situation in which approximation would be appropriate would be if you were asked to figure out how many people exist in the world. It would be almost impossible to know the exact figure, but an approximate answer would give you a good idea of the answer. Another way to say you are approximating something is to **estimate** it.

Area – The amount of **two-dimensional** space an object covers is referred to as its area. In its simplest form, area can be thought of as the length of the object multiplied by its width. The **units of measurement** used to express area are always some form of a square unit, such as square inches or square meters. The most common abbreviation for area is A.

Associative Property – For any numbers a, b, and c, in addition: (a + b) + c = a + (b + c); for multiplication: (a x b) x c = a x (b x c).

Average – The **sum** of a **set** of numbers divided by the total number of items in the set. For example, the average of the numbers 1, 2, and 6 is (1 + 2 + 6)/3, which equals 3.

Bar Graph – A graph containing rectangular bars whose lengths correspond to a specific amount of **data**. (see example on page 156)

Base – In a **three-dimensional** object, the **face** around which the object is formed. For example, the base of a triangular **prism** is a **triangle** and the base of a square **pyramid** is a **square**.

Circle – A circle is formed by using a fixed, imaginary point as a starting point or center, and then recording the points around it that are all equal in distance from it. The distance from the center of a circle to its **perimeter** is called the **radius**. The line which travels through the center and divides the circle in half is called the **diameter**; it is equal to twice the length of the radius. The perimeter or **circumference** of a circle is found by multiplying the length of the diameter by **pi** (π), which is approximately equal to 3.14 (C = π x d). The **area** of a circle is found by multiplying pi (3.14) by the squared length of the radius (A = π x r²). In terms of degrees, the number of degrees traveled from a point on a circle back to itself is 360. (see example page 154)

Circumference – In a **circle**, the length of the **perimeter** is known as the circle's circumference. The formula for circumference is **pi** times the length of the **diameter** (C = π x d).

Commutative Property – For any numbers a and b, in addition: a + b = b + a; in multiplication: a x b = b x a.

Compare – To examine the similarities, differences, and/or values of two or more numbers or objects. For example, students may be asked to compare the equations 2 + 4 = n and 1 + 6 = y and decide whether y is greater than n, which it is. Students may also be asked to compare two **triangles** and decide if they are **congruent**, **similar**, or neither.

Compass – An instrument, consisting of an anchor point and a pencil, used to construct geometric shapes, especially **circles**.

Composite Number – A number that has two or more **factors** is called a composite number. Examples include 4, 35, and 121. The numbers zero and one are **not** composite numbers. (see **Prime Number**)

Cone – A cone is a special type of **pyramid** with a circular base. An example of a cone is an ice cream cone. (see example page 155)

Congruent – Any two figures or measurements which are equal in size or value are referred to as congruent. Congruency applies to the lengths of sides of **polygons** or **angle** measures. It also applies to polygons as a whole. For example, two **squares** with sides equal in length are said to be congruent to one another. (see **Similar**)

Coordinate – The numerical value of the location of a **point** on a **graph**.

Cross-multiply – A method used for evaluating whether **fractions** are equal. It can be utilized when you have two fractions that are on opposite sides of an equation. For example, if you are asked whether or not 3/4 equals 219/292, you can set them equal to one another and cross multiply: 3/4 = 219/292. To cross-multiply, simply multiply each **numerator** by the **denominator** of the other fraction, and drop the original denominator: 3 x 292 = 4 x 219. After evaluating these numbers, you see that: 876 = 876. Yes, these fractions are equal. Cross-multiplication is especially useful when working with **proportions** and **ratios**. For example, if there are 4 oranges for every 5 apples, how many oranges (n) are there if there are 95 apples. To solve this, set up an **equation** using the original ratio and the unknown one: 4/5 = n/95. Cross-multiply to get: 380 = 5n. After you divide each side by 5, you find the number of oranges is 76.

Cube – A **three-dimensional** object with 12 **edges** and 6 **faces** that are all **congruent squares**. A cube is a special type of **prism**. The **volume** of a cube is found by multiplying its length times its width times its height (V = l x w x h). An example of a cube is a die. (see example page 155)

Cylinder – A special type of **prism** with a **circle**, instead of a **polygon**, for a **base**. An example of a cylinder is a can. (see example page 155)

Data – A **set** of given information.

Decimal – A decimal is another method of expressing **rational numbers**. Numbers that are **integers** and numbers that are not integers can both be written as decimals. For example, 1 can be written as a decimal in the form 1.0; 1/2 can be written as a decimal in the form 0.5; 3 4/5 can be written as a deci-mal in the form 3.8. Anything to the right of the decimal point represents a value less than 1. The greater the number to the right of the decimal point, the greater the number is. For example, 0.98 is greater than 0.13; 0.67 is greater than 0.089 (think of this as 0.670 compared to 0.089, or 670 is greater than 89). However, the number 3.1 is greater than 0.9 because the number to the left of the decimal point must always be included when comparing decimals. (see **Place Value**)

Denominator – In a **fraction**, the number below the fraction bar ("the bottom number"). In the case of 1/4, for example, the denominator is 4.

Diameter – In a **circle**, the line which travels through its center from one edge of the circle to the other, and divides the circle in half. The length of the diameter is twice the length of the **radius**.

Difference – The **solution** to an **equation** involving subtraction.

Direct Proportion – A method of comparing two equal **ratios**. For example, if for every 3 people there are 2 dogs, how many dogs will there be for 9 people? The direct proportion to solve this sets the origi-nal/known ratio of people to dogs equal to the unknown ratio: 3/2 = 9/n or 3/2 = 9/6. In this example, the answer derived from the direct proportion is 6.

Distributive Property – For any number a, b, and c: a x (b + c) = a x b + a x c.

Edge – In **three-dimensional** objects, any of the **segments** that define the shape of the **faces** of the object. Edges make up the **perimeter** of each face and the object as a whole. In a **cube**, for example, there are 12 edges.

Equation – Any expression which sets two or more things equal to one another is an equation. An equation can be recognized by the presence of an equals sign (=).

Equiangular – In any given **polygon**, if the measures of all the **angles** formed by the figure's seg-ments are of equal value (**congruent**), the polygon is said to be equiangular. All **regular polygons** are equiangular. Not all equiangular polygons are necessarily **equilateral**.

Equilateral – In any given **polygon**, if the lengths of all of the sides are of equal value (**congruent**), the polygon is said to be equilateral. All **regular polygons** are equilateral. All equilateral polygons are also **equiangular**.

Estimate – see **Approximate**; **Rounding**.

Exponent – When a number is raised to a **power**, the power it is raised to is expressed by using an exponent. The exponent shows how many times a number is to be multiplied by itself. An exponent can be any **rational number**, but for the purpose of the WASL, exponents will only include whole numbers greater than zero. When written, exponents appear after the number they influence, and are slightly raised above the number, such as 2^3 or 4^2: $2^3 = 2 \times 2 \times 2$ and $4^2 = 4 \times 4$.

Face – In **three-dimensional** objects, the shape that makes up one surface or **side** of the object. For example, in a **cube**, there are 6 faces, all of which are **squares**.

Factor – Any integer you can evenly divide into another number is a factor of that number. The complete **set** of factors for the number 24 is {1, 2, 3, 4, 6, 8, 12, 24}. An important aspect of factors is being able to find the **prime numbers** that are factors of other numbers. Prime   factors break down a number into its most basic parts. Again, use 24 as an example. The prime factors of 24 are $2 \times 2 \times 2 \times 3$. This can be seen by taking other factor pairs of 24, such as 4 and 6, and breaking them down into primes: $(2 \times 2) \times (2 \times 3)$. (see **Multiple**)

Flip – When asked to flip an object, students are being asked to move the object around an imaginary line. The object will maintain its shape, but will be facing a different direction after the flip (mirrored of what it was originally). This process is called **reflection**. (see example on page 157)

Fraction – A method of expressing **rational numbers**, **ratios**, and division. Fractions are written in the form a/b, where a is the **numerator** and b is the **denominator**. Numbers that are **integers** can be expressed as fractions, such as 3: 3/1. Numbers that are not integers can also be expressed as fractions, such as 0.25: 1/4. Fractions can be either **proper** or **improper**.

Graph – A visual method of presenting numerical **data** or **equations**. Some examples of types of graphs are coordinate **line graphs**, **pie charts**, **bar graphs**, **histograms**, **scatterplots**, and **pictographs**. (see examples on page 156)

Grid – The **intersecting** lines which make up a **graph**. A grid is used to help **plot points**.

Hexagon – A **polygon** with exactly 6 **sides**. The total measure of the **angles** within a hexagon is 720°.

Histogram – A **graph**, similar to a **bar graph**, containing rectangular bars whose lengths and widths correspond to a specific amount of **data**. (see example on page 156)

Identity Property – In multiplication, for any number a: $a \times 1 = a$.

Improper Fraction – Any fraction in which the **numerator** is greater than the **denominator** is called an improper fraction. All improper fractions can be converted to **mixed numbers**. By definition, the value of all improper fractions is greater than or equal to 1. Examples of improper fractions include 9/5, 26/11, or 100/10.

Inequality – Any expression which denotes two or more things are not equal to one another is an inequality. There are a number of specific inequality types including less than (<), greater than (>), and not equal to (≠).

Integer – Any number, positive or negative, that is a **whole number** distance away from zero on a number line, in addition to zero. Specifically, an integer is any number in the **set** {...-3, -2, -1, 0, 1, 2, 3...}. Examples of integers include 1, 5, 273, -2, -35, and –1,375. Numbers that are not integers are **fractions** or **decimals** that do not equal whole numbers, such as 1/2, 2.34, -3/7, and -10.25.

Intersect – Two lines or **segments** that cross at any given point are said to intersect. Figures, such as **polygons**, are formed by intersecting segments.

Isosceles Triangle – A **triangle** with exactly two **sides** of equal length. (see example page 154)

Line Graph – A graph based on an **equation**, such as $3x + 1 = y$, which is **plotted** on a **grid** using an **x-axis** and **y-axis**. (see example on page 156)

Line of Symmetry – A line, real or imaginary, that divides an object into two **congruent** parts. A **square**, for example, has four lines of symmetry (one vertical; one horizontal; two diagonal).

Mean – The mean of a **set** of numbers is simply the **average** of the numbers given. For example, in the set {1, 2, 4, 6, 17}, the mean is $(1 + 2 + 4 + 6 + 17)/5$, which equals 6. The mean does not have to be a number which appears in the original set. For example, the mean of the set {1, 5, 12} is $(1 + 5 +12)/3$, which equals 6.

Median – In any given **set** of numbers arranged by ascending or descending value, the number which is the exact middle term of the set. For example, in a set of 11 numbers, the sixth term would by the median because it is exactly half way from the beginning and end of the set. In the set {2, 3, 6, 12, 451}, the median is 6, because it is the third term in the set of 5 numbers. For sets of numbers with an even number of terms, the median is the **average** of the two middle terms. For example, in the set {0, 2, 3, 4, 19, 78}, the median is the average of the third and fourth terms because it is a 6-term set. In this case, the median is 3.5.

Metric System – A **decimal** system of weights and measurements based on the meter and kilogram. For the purpose of the WASL, students need not know the relationship between units within the metric system but should be able to identify and use units in proper measurements. The following is a list of the base units of the metric system, as well as a few of their more common derivatives and abbreviations: length — millimeter, centimeter, meter, kilometer (mm., cm., m., km.); volume — cubic centimeter, milliliter, liter (cu. cm., ml., l.); weight — grams, kilograms g., kg.); temperature — degrees Celsius (ºC); time — second, minute, hour, day, week, month, year. (see **U.S. System**)

Mixed Number – Any **rational number** greater than or equal to 1 can be expressed as a mixed number, that is in the form of an **integer** and a **proper fraction**. Mixed numbers are oftentimes derived from **improper fractions** (all mixed numbers can be written as improper fractions, and vice versa). An example is 7/4, which, when written as a mixed number, is 1 3/4. To convert an improper fraction to a mixed number, first divide the **numerator** by the **denominator**. In the case of 7/4, 4 goes into 7 only once. One becomes the integer portion of the mixed number. Next, take the remainder from the division and make it the numerator of the proper fraction portion of the mixed number, in this case, 3. Finally, simply use the denominator of the improper fraction as the denominator of the proper fraction, which is 4. By doing this, we see the 7/4 is the same as saying 1 3/4. An easy way to tell whether or not an improper fraction equals a mixed number is to find the decimal value of each; they should be equal.

Mode – In any given **set** of numbers, the mode is the number that occurs most often. For example, in the set {1, 2, 2, 3, 3, 4, 4, 4}, the mode is 4. If more than one number occurs the greatest number of times, there are multiple modes. For example, in the set {1, 1, 2, 2, 3}, the modes are 1 and 2. Unlike **mean** and **median,** the mode of a set is always a number that occurs somewhere in the set.

Multiple – Any number which is the product of two integers is said to be a multiple of those numbers. For example, some multiples of the number 4 are 8, 12, 36, and 4,000, which are (4 x 2), (4 x 3), (4 x 9), and (4 x 1,000), respectively. In each case, the number is a multiple of 4, while individually, the products are multiples of both 4 and 2, 4 and 3, 4 and 9, and 4 and 1,000, respectively. (see **Factor**)

Numerator – In a **fraction,** the number which appears above the fraction bar (the "top number"). In the fraction 5/8 for example, the numerator is 5.

Obtuse – An **angle** with a measure greater than 90°.

Octagon – A **polygon** with exactly 8 sides. The total measure of the **angles** within an octagon is 1080°.

Order of Operations – When solving any **equation**, there is a proper order of operations to consider: parentheses, **exponents**, multiplication, division, addition, subtraction. An easy way to remember this is by using the mnemonic device "Please excuse my dear Aunt Sally" or PEMDAS. For an example of proper order of operations, consider the following: $(40 + 40)/2 - 2^2$ x 3. Students would first do the math inside the parentheses, resulting in $80/2 - 2^2$ x 3. Next, students would raise the 2 by a **power** of 2: $80/2 - 4$ x 3. Multiplication is next: 80/2 – 12. Then division, 40 – 24. Finally, because there is no addition left to do, subtract: 28.

Ordered Pair – see **Point**.

Parallel – When two lines or **segments** travel in such a way that they will never **intersect** if continued, they are said to be parallel to one another. The **symbol** denoting parallel lines is ‖.

Parallelogram – A **quadrilateral** with both pairs of opposite sides **parallel** to one another. Each side is equal in length to the side opposite it. The **area** of a parallelogram is found by multiplying the length of the base by the length of the height (A = b x h). Special cases of parallelograms include **rectangles** and **rhombi**. (see example page 154)

Pattern – A repeatable occurrence in a given **set** or **sequence** of numbers or figures. In the sequence {1, 2, 3, 4, 5...}, for example, the pattern is to add 1 to the number to obtain the next number in the sequence. A pattern is sometimes referred to as a **trend**.

Pentagon – A **polygon** with exactly 5 sides. The total measure of the **angles** within a pentagon is 540°.

Percent – When you take a specific part of a value, this is referred to as taking a percent of the original value. Percent literally means "per hundred," and is represented by the **symbol** %. Any given percent can be written fractionally as that number over a **denominator** of 100 (all percents can be expressed as **fractions**, and vice versa). For example, the expression 25% can be thought of fractionally as 25/100 or 1/4. Percents are useful because they can be used as **direct proportions**. For example, if you want to know what 75% of 576 is, set up the following proportion: 75/100 = n/576. You could also evaluate this by changing 75% into its equivalent fraction, 3/4, and multiplying by 576: 3/4 x 576. Percents are also used to represent **probability.**

Perimeter – The total length of the outside border of an object is called its perimeter. For any **polygon**, the actual value is found by finding the sum of the lengths of all of its sides. For example, a triangle with sides of 5 inches, 4 inches, and 3 inches has a perimeter of 12 inches. The **units of measurement** used to express perimeter are linear units, such as inches or kilometers. The most common abbreviation for perimeter is P.

Perpendicular – When two lines or **segments intersect** and form **right angles**, they are said to be perpendicular to one another. The **symbol** for perpendicular is ⊥ .

Pi – A number that expresses the **ratio** of the **circumference** of a **circle** to its **diameter**. It is represented by the **symbol** π, and is used in circles to find both **area** and **perimeter**. Pi is approximately equal to 3.14 or 22/7.

Pictograph – A graph that represents **data** using pictures rather than lines or numbers. A pictograph always has a corresponding key to tell what information the picture represents. (see example on page 156)

Pie Chart – A type of **graph** usually used to represent **percents**. Its layout is circular, and **data** is given appropriately sized wedges of the circle based on their corresponding percents. (see example on page 156)

Place Value – The location of a specific digit in any given number. Consider the following number for a description of specific place values: 1,234,567.890. The 1 is in the millions place; the 2 is in the hundred thousands place; the 3 is in the ten thousands place; the 4 is in the thousands place; the 5 is in the hundreds place; the 6 is in the tens place; the 7 is in the ones place; the 8 is in the tenths place; the 9 is in the hundredths place; and, the 0 is in the thousandths place.

Place value is essential when comparing the size of numbers. When comparing numbers, first look at the leftmost digit of each number. The number with a digit in the leftmost place value is greater. If both numbers have digits in that place value, the number with the greater digit in that place value is greater.

Plot – To place **points** at their proper **coordinates** on a **graph**.

Point – A location on a **graph** defined by its position in relation to the **x-axis** and **y-axis**. Points are sometimes called **ordered pairs** and are written in this form: (x-**coordinate**, y-coordinate).

Polygon – A closed **two-dimensional** figure of three or more sides formed by segments that meet only at their endpoints; no more than two segments meet at any given endpoint. Examples of polygons include **triangles**, **rectangles**, **parallelograms**, **pentagons**, **hexagons**, and **octagons**. A general formula to find the sum of **angles** for any polygon is to subtract the number of sides by 2; then, multiply this number by 180° (sum of angles = (n – 2) x 180°). Special polygons that have sides of equal length are called **regular polygons**. (For examples, see page 154)

Power – When a number is raised by an **exponent**, it is said to be raised by that power. For example, 3^4 can be thought of as the fourth power of three. To find the actual value, the base number, in this case 3, is multiplied by itself a number of times equal to the value of the exponent, in this case, 4: 3 x 3 x 3 x 3. Therefore, three to the fourth power equals 81.

Precision – How close a set of trials or values are in relationship to one another. Consider again the example of the dartboard. Suppose you are again aiming for the 20 at the top of the board. You throw three darts, all of which hit the number 2, which is on the opposite side of the board. Although, the darts were nowhere near their intended target, and, therefore, not very **accurate**; but, because they all hit relatively the same point, we can say that the throws were extremely precise. (see **Accuracy**)

Predict – To make a guess based on known information and observation. For example, if you are given the **sequence** of numbers {2, 4, 6, 8,…}, you could predict, based on an observed **pattern**, that the next number in the sequence is 10.

Prime Number – A number that is not divisible by any numbers other than itself and the number one is referred to as prime. Prime numbers are the **factors** of **composite numbers** (numbers that are not prime). Examples of prime numbers include 13, 23, and 61. The numbers zero and one are **not** prime numbers; the only even prime number is 2. Prime numbers cannot be negative.

Prism – A **three-dimensional** object formed connecting the corresponding **vertexes** of two **congruent**, **parallel faces** that are **polygons**. The **volume** of any prism is found by multiplying its length times it width times its height (V = l x w x h). (see example page 155)

Probability – The likelihood that an event will occur. Specifically, probability is the number of desired events divided by the number of possible outcomes. For example, when finding the probability of flipping a coin and having it land on heads, the number of desired events equals 1, and the number of possible outcomes equals 2. Probability is most often recorded in **ratios** or **percents**; therefore, in the example, the probability of flipping a coin and having it land on heads is 1:2, or 1/2, or 50%.

Product – The **solution** to an **equation** involving multiplication.

Proper Fraction – Any fraction with the **numerator** less than or equal to the **denominator** is called a proper fraction. By definition, the value of all proper fractions is less than or equal to 1. Examples of proper fractions include 1/2, 5/16, 786/5563, and 2/2.

Properties – Known interactions of numbers in specific situations in addition and multiplication. (see **Associative Property, Commutative Property, Distributive Property, Identity Property, and Zero Property**)

Proportion – see **Direct Proportion**.

Protractor – An instrument used to measure **angles** of geometric shapes. Most protractors measure up to 180º, which is the measure of a straight line.

Pyramid – A **three-dimensional** figure with a **polygon** for a base, with the rest of the **faces** formed by forming **segments** from each **vertex** of the polygon to a common vertex away from the base. An example of a pyramid is some circus tents. (see example page 155)

Quadrilateral – Any **polygon** with exactly four sides is called a quadrilateral. Some types of quadrilaterals have special names and properties, including **rectangles**, **squares**, **parallelograms**, **rhombi**, and **trapezoids**.

Quotient – The **solution** to an **equation** involving division.

Radius – The length from the center of a **circle** to its **perimeter**. The value of the radius is equal to half the length of the **diameter**.

Range – In a **set** of numbers, the two extremes in the set; in other words, the minimum and maximum values in a set. For example, the range of the set {2, 5, 8, 23, 46} is 2 to 46.

Rate – A rate is an expression of how long it takes to do something. Examples of rates are miles per hour and revolutions per minute. In general, rate is measured as an event divided by a unit of time.

Ratio – A ratio is a comparison of two numbers. Ratios can be expressed in one of the following ways: 3/1, or 3:1, or 3 to 1. In this example, all the ratios are equal. Ratios can be used to compare like and different items. For example, a ratio may indicate that for every 3 apples grown, 1 was eaten; or, for every 3 apples grown, 1 orange was also grown. Ratios are also used to express **direct proportions** and **probability**.

Rational Number – A number that can be formed as the **ratio** of two **integers**. Examples include 2 (written as a ratio: 2/1), 0.5 (written as a ratio: 1/2), and 1.75 (written as a ratio: 7/4).

Rectangle – A **quadrilateral** with each pair of opposite sides parallel to one another and whose sides meet at **right angles**. A rectangle is a special type of **parallelogram**. A **square** is a special type of rectangle. The **area** of a rectangle is found by multiplying its length by its width (A = l $\times$ w). (see example page 154)

Reflection – see **Flip**.

Regular polygons – A special type of **polygon** that is both **equilateral** and **equiangular**.

Rhombus – A rhombus is a **quadrilateral,** and more specifically, a special type of **parallelogram** having four sides of equal length with each pair of opposite sides **parallel** to each other. The **area** of a rhombus is found by multiplying the length of the base by the length of the height (A = b $\times$ h). A special type of rhombus is a **square**. (see example page 154)

Right Angle – An **angle** with a measure of exactly 90°. The lines or **segments** which form right angles are said to be **perpendicular** to one another.

Rotation – see **Turn**.

Rounding – Taking an exact value and making it an **approximation**. Rounding is done by examining the value of the number in the **place value** to the right of the place value to which you want to round. If this number is less than 5 in value, you round down; if it is equal to 5 or greater, you round up. To round the number 114 to the nearest ten, you first examine the number in the ones place because it is to the right of the tens place. Because this number is less than 5, you round down to the nearest ten. To do this, look at the numbers that make up the places up to and including the place you want to round to, in this case, the tens place. The number is 14, so you round down to the nearest ten, which is 10. The value of 114 rounded to the nearest ten is therefore 110. For another example, round 368 to the nearest ten. Since the ones place is occupied by a number greater than 5, you round up in this situation. The nearest ten up from this number is 370. Finally, round the number 10.35 to the nearest tenth. Because the number to the right of the tenths place is equal to 5, you must round up. The nearest tenth rounded up, in this situation, is 10.40. Rounding can be done for numbers in any place value.

Ruler – A straight-edged instrument used for measuring the lengths of objects. A ruler usually has inches or centimeters for its units.

Scatterplot – A type of **graph** containing **points** similar to a line graph, except the points are not contained within one specific **equation**. This type of graph is usually used when data seems more random than ordered. (see example on page 156)

Segment - A line ending at specific points. Segments meet at vertexes to form closed figures, both two- and three-dimensional.

Semicircle – Half of a **circle** with the **diameter** as its base.

Sequence – Any ordered **set** of numbers or objects produced by an observable **pattern** is called a sequence. Perhaps the most basic sequence of numbers is the numbers used when counting: 1, 2, 3, 4, 5,…. A definite pattern can be seen, and we can **predict** how the sequence will continue. Another example of a numerical sequence is: 1, 1, 1, 1, 1, 1…. Although the numbers in the set never change, we can observe this as a pattern, and thus determine that the sequence will continue in a similar fashion. Sequences can also include geometric shapes. For example, if you see a **triangle** followed by a **square** followed by a triangle followed by a square, you can safely assume that this is a sequence, which will continue with a triangle.

Set – Any grouping of numbers. A set can be specific or random, small or large. Sets are usually notated by placing numbers within brackets, such as {1, 2, 3}. Before finding statistical **data** of sets, you should always arrange the values in descending or ascending order.

Side – In any **polygon**, a segment which is part of its construction. The number of sides helps define the specific type of polygon. Some examples include **triangles**, which have 3 sides, **quadrilaterals**, which have 4 sides, and **pentagons**, which have 5 sides. In **three-dimensional** figures, the word "side" is often used to refer to the **face** of the object.

Similar – Two **polygons** are said to be similar to one another if they have an equal number of sides with corresponding **angles** of equal measure. For example, all **squares** are similar to each other, but not necessarily **congruent**, because by definition all squares have four **right angles.** Figures whose definitions do not rely on angle measure are not necessarily similar. For example, although **triangles** can be similar or congruent, they do not have to be because the measures of their angles can vary (an **equilateral** triangle is neither congruent nor similar to a **right triangle**).

Simplify – To take a given mathematical expression and put it into its most basic form while keeping it equal to its original value. To simplify 4/2, for example, you would change it to 2, because they are equal to one another. To simplify the **equation** 3n + 2n + 2 + 1 = 0, you would combine the like terms and get 5n + 3 = 0. Simplifying does not necessarily require a specific value to be obtained and should not be confused with **solving.**

Slide – When asked to slide an object, students are being asked to move it a certain distance while maintaining the size and orientation (direction) of the object. This is known as **translation**. (see example on page 157)

Solution – The answer to an equation that is being solved.

Solve – A term used when evaluating **equations**, **variables**, and **unknowns**. To solve the equation 3 + 3 = n, the value of the unknown n is the **solution**, which in this case is 6. When working with variables, an equation's solution is dependent on the value of one of the variables. For example, if given the equation n –1 = y, students may be asked to solve for y if n = 2. In this case, the solution is 1.

Sphere – A **three-dimensional** object formed by taking a **radius** of given length and revolving it three-dimensionally around a given point. The shape formed represents any area that the radius may possibly travel through. An example of a sphere is a baseball. (see example page 153)

Square – A **quadrilateral** with each pair of opposite sides **parallel** to one another, all sides equal in length, and sides that meet at **right angles.** By definition, a square is also a **rectangle**, a **parallelogram**, and a **rhombus.** The **area** of a square is found by multiplying its length by its width (A = l x w). (see example page 154)

Sum – The **solution** to an **equation** involving addition.

Symbol – A symbol is a method of representing a number or **unknown** value and/or words by using other characters. Symbols can be letters, as they often are for unknowns and **variables**, and they can also be specialized characters, such as $, which means dollars, or >, which means greater than.

Symmetric – An object is said to exhibit symmetry if it is possible to split the object with any line, real or imaginary (see **Line of Symmetry**), and produce two new objects of exact attributes. For example, in a **circle**, the **diameter** divides the circle into two equal **semicircles**. These semicircles are symmetric because they are equal in relation to the diameter. If you divide a **square** in half, it also exhibits symmetry. However, in a **rectangle**, for example, symmetry is only exhibited when the lines are drawn horizontally or vertically through the center of the rectangle. Although drawing a line diagonally through the center produces two equal (**congruent**) halves, they are not symmetrical around the line. A good way to picture symmetry is to draw a line through an object and mentally fold the object on that line. If the two halves match up exactly, the figure is symmetrical.

Three-dimensional – Having measurable properties of length, width, and height. (see figures on page 155)

Translation – see **Slide**.

Trapezoid – A special type of **quadrilateral** with only one pair of opposite **sides parallel** to one another. The **area** of a trapezoid is found by multiplying the **sum** of its parallel sides by its height, then dividing by two (A = [h(sum of parallel sides)/2]). (see example page 154)

Trend – see **Pattern**.

Triangle – Any **polygon** having exactly three sides is called a triangle. The sum of the **angles** of a triangle is always equal to 180°. To find the area of any triangle, multiply the length of the base by the length of the height; then, divide by 2; A = (b $\times$ h)/2. Some special types of triangles include **equilateral**, **isosceles**, and **right triangles**. (see example page 154)

Turn – When asked to turn an object, students are being asked to move the object around an imaginary point in a circular motion. After the move, the object will have the same shape and size, but will be facing a different direction. This is also known as **rotation**. (see example on page 157)

Two-dimensional – Having measurable properties of length and width, only. (see figures on page 154)

U.S. System of Measurement – This is the system of measurement that most people in the United States still use, while the rest of the world, for the most part, uses the **metric system**. The following is a list of common U.S. units of measurement with their abbreviations: length — inches, feet, yards, miles (in., ft., yd., mi.,); volume — fluid ounces, teaspoons, tablespoons, cups, pint, quarts, gallons (fl. oz., tsp., tbsp., pt., qt., gal.); weight — ounces, pounds, tons (oz., lb., t.); temperature — degrees Fahrenheit (°F); time — second, minute, hour, day, week, month, year.

Units of Measurement – Units of measurement are used to record how specific values relate to the objects from which they were taken. Units not only give clues as to what type of measurement is being made, but also relate to the size of the measurement. For example, if a measurement is recorded as 5 inches, you know the measurement is an object's length. If a measurement is 1 mile, even though the number is small, you know this is a relatively large distance.

When recording units of measurement, there are two common systems that are utilized: the **U.S. system** and the **metric system**. Each system has its own units which students must be able to recognize and use. Common attributes of an object which are measured include length, volume, weight, speed, temperature, and time. Although it is not necessary for students to memorize the conversions from one system to the other, they should be able to recognize units of similar size. For example, pounds would be used in the same situation as kilograms, but most likely not grams; for grams, the similar unit might be ounces. Students should also be able to identify units of measurement based on common abbreviations, such as in. for inches or m. for meters.

Unknown – The part of an **equation** which is not known and must be solved for. Unknowns can be represented by letters or other **symbols**. For example, in the equation 2n = 6, the unknown is represented by the letter "n." The value of the unknown, in this case, is 3.

Variable – In an **equation**, a value which can change and affect the overall value of the expression. Variables are represented by using letters such as "*n*" or "*y*." For example, in the equation 3n + 1 = y, the value of y will vary as the value of n changes, and vice versa. If n = 1, then y = 4, but if n = 3, y = 10. Variables are a special type of **unknown** which are always dependent on other variables.

Vertex – In a **three-dimensional** object, any point where three or more **segments** join to form a corner of the object. In a **cube**, for example, there are 8 vertexes.

Volume – The amount of area taken up by a **three-dimensional** object is known as its volume. In its simplest expression, volume is an object's length multiplied by its width multiplied by its height/depth. The **units of measurement** used to express volume can be cubic units, such as cubic feet or cubic centimeters, or, when measuring fluids, units such as gallons or liters. Volume is usually abbreviated as V.

Whole Number – An **integer** in the **set** {0, 1, 2, 3…}. In other words, a whole number is any number used when counting, in addition to zero.

X-axis – On a **graph**, the number line which runs horizontally. (see example on page 156)

Y-axis – On a **graph**, the number line which runs vertically. (see example on page 156)

Zero Property – For any number a, in addition: a + 0 = a; in multiplication: a x 0 = 0.

Examples of Common Two-Dimensional Geometric Shapes

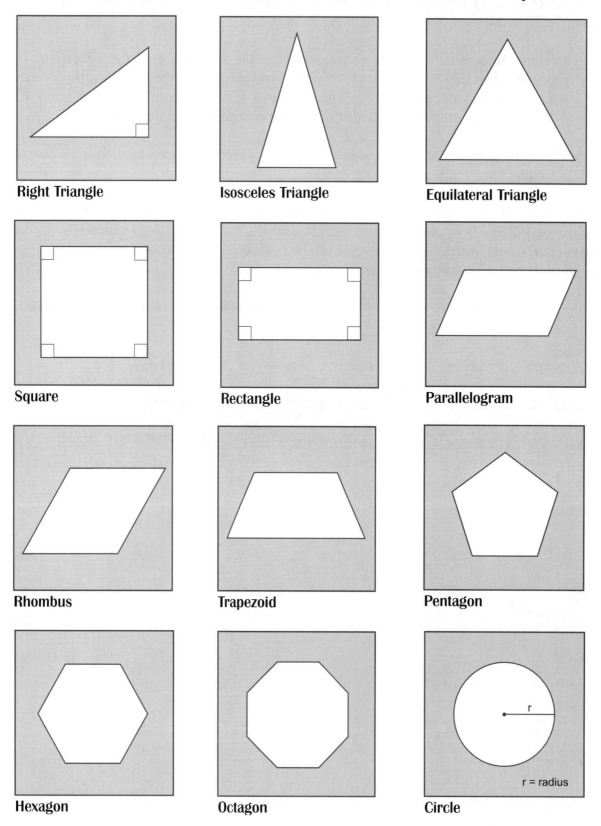

Right Triangle

Isosceles Triangle

Equilateral Triangle

Square

Rectangle

Parallelogram

Rhombus

Trapezoid

Pentagon

Hexagon

Octagon

Circle

r = radius

Examples of Common Three—Dimensional Objects

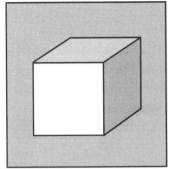

Cube

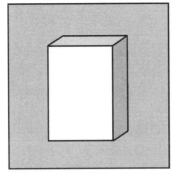

Rectangular Prism

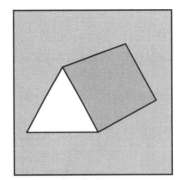

Triangular Prism

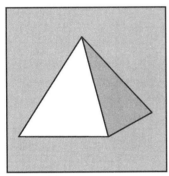

Pyramid

Cylinder

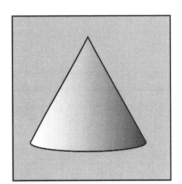

Cone

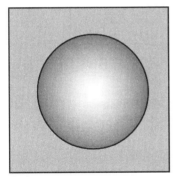

Sphere

Example Shapes

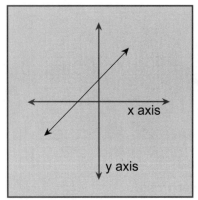

Line Graph

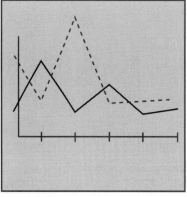

Double Line Graph

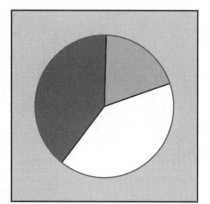

Pie Chart

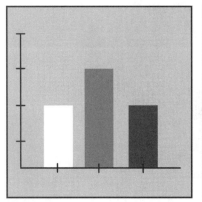

Histogram

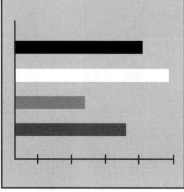

Bar Graph

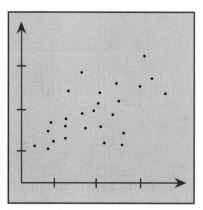

Scatterplot

Pictograph

Stem and Leaf Plot

Examples of Object Movement

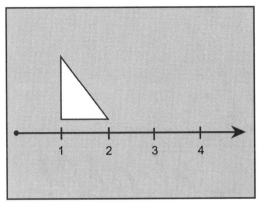 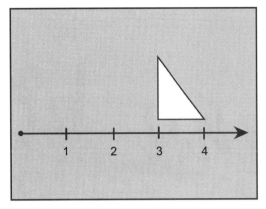

Slide (Translation)

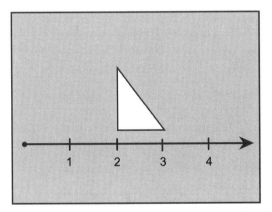 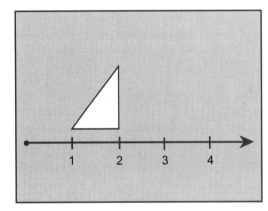

Flip (Reflection)

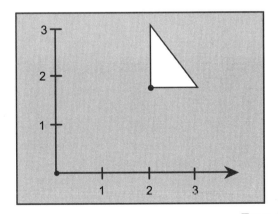 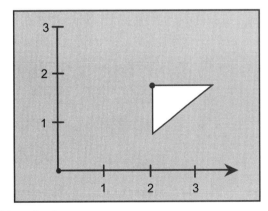

Turn (Rotation)

Thank YOU
For Your Purchase!

For more information on WASL products,

call 1-877-PASSING (727-7464), or

visit our website:

www.passthewasl.com